WITHDRAWN

Sociology Noir

Sociology Noir

Studies at the University
of Chicago in Loneliness,
Marginality and Deviance,
1915–1935

ROGER A. SALERNO

McFarland & Company, Inc., Publishers

Jefferson, North Carolina, and London

LIBRARY OF CONGRESS CATALOGUING-IN-PUBLICATION DATA

Salerno, Roger, A.
    Sociology noir : studies at the University of Chicago in
loneliness, marginality and deviance, 1915–1935 / Roger A.
Salerno.
        p.   cm.
    Includes bibliographical references and index.

    ISBN-13: 978-0-7864-2990-5
    softcover : 50# alkaline paper ∞

    1. Chicago school of sociology—History.   2. Sociology—
United States—History.   I. Title.
HM477.U6S27   2007
301.09773'11—dc22   2007011131

British Library cataloguing data are available

Cover photograph ©2006 PhotoSpin

Manufactured in the United States of America

McFarland & Company, Inc., Publishers
    Box 611, Jefferson, North Carolina 28640
    www.mcfarlandpub.com

Contents

For Sandi

Preface

THERE ARE POINTS AT WHICH SOCIOLOGY and popular culture collide to produce remarkably informative and entertaining prose. Between 1915 and 1935 the University of Chicago was the center for the production of innovative sociological research that resonated with the lives of urban Americans. Referred to as the Chicago school monographs by historians and scholars, these works brought acclaim to the graduate program in sociology at the University of Chicago and made it truly exceptional. For the most part, these were studies conducted on the social margins of urban life—up-close studies of delinquents, prostitutes, gangsters, and homeless men.

The Chicago school monographs were constructed by young men and women who were fascinated by the world in which they lived—a diverse urban world surrounding the university they attended. Through their fieldwork they sought to understand it as well as to personally connect to it in some ways.

This book is a survey of some of the key monographs of the Chicago school of sociology and the men who produced them. The purpose of this work is no more ambitious than to point out that there are aspects of this American sociology that resonated with the culture of the day, focused on the drama of marginality of city life and used some of the same techniques as reportage and literature to make their points. I have referred to this work as Sociology *Noir*; and by doing so I use the term *noir* in the broadest possible way. I am not saying here that this sociology shares the same world view as American roman noir, which for the most part was much more pessimistic and cynical than that shared by these sociologists. But what I am saying is that there was a popular romance with marginality at this time, and a new openness about sex, gender, and deviance—or at least a greater awareness and recognition of their importance. While these interests were characteristic of literary genres of this era, they were central to urban sociology.

I have no illusion that this is a great in-depth survey of the Chicago school on the scale of Martin Bulmer's classic *The Chicago School of Sociology* (1983), Rolf Lindner's *Reportage of Urban Culture* (1996), or Andrew Abbott's *Department and Discipline* (2002). I have relied heavily on these works to help construct my own reading of the events that I've laid out here. Particularly important to me as a source of inspiration was Carla Cappetti's *Writing Chicago* (1993), an amazing work on the relationship between Chicago sociology and American proletarian fiction. I must say that reading her book made me want to return to the subject of my doctoral dissertation with a new perspective.

Feminists, among whose ranks I count myself, might have some difficulties with this volume. Where are the women? Well, there were many, but their light was eclipsed by the institutional phallocentrism at the university at the time and the unwillingness of the press to recognize their contributions (Deegan, 1988). The same might be said for women who worked in the genres of proletarian and hard-boiled fiction. Only a few were truly appreciated. Olive Tilford Dargan (whose pseudonym was Fielding Burke), Tillie Olsen, Meridel LeSueur, and others helped shape the 1930s view on the domestic oppression of women and capital's exploitation of their labor. Dorothy Hughes and Georgiana Ann Randolph Craig gained a significant reputation in the hard-boiled genre. But even Craig, one of the most brilliant hard-boiled Chicago-based writers, was forced to use a male pseudonym, Craig Rice, to sell her books.

The importance of sociology as a narrative is underscored here. In some sense, it is the narrative of sociology that speaks to the broader culture and maintains an ongoing dialogue with it. We understand from the narratives reviewed that hard-boiled fiction, proletarian prose, and journalistic excursions into the mean streets of the city have much in common with urban sociology of this era. In the early twentieth century marginality is first being discovered as something quite central to American life. Sex and violence are becoming more explicit and less hidden. The dark city becomes the new frontier; tales of urban crime, aloneness, and estrangement begin to displace those of the Western adventure.

2

This work is an expedition through some of these dark ethnographies of the city streets. It is hoped that from this underworld excursion a better understanding might be grasped of the value and significance of Chicago school sociology and the people who helped to create it.

Reconstructing history is a difficult task. This is especially true for the nonhistorian. It is so much easier to secure details if your sources are living, or if there are people still around who were close to the events. Nevertheless, I do make the point that facts are not always clear and memories are never objective. What people left behind, which allows us to reconstruct events, is not always as informative as we'd like.

While there was an array of official and unofficial documents available that would have helped to illustrate points in this work, official sources were frequently noncooperative. This was particularly true for the FBI, which claimed that it had no files on the W.I. Thomas case despite newspaper accounts of its active involvement with it at the time. I have also found that news organizations frequently cooperated with the FBI and the federal district attorney in the past. But stonewalling and collusion speak volumes. I will not go into them any further here.

Those who were invaluable in my work were the Special Collections Division of the Regenstein Library at the University of Chicago, Michelle Fannelli at the Burnbaum Library at Pace, and a host of personal contacts who attempted to help me piece together a more or less accurate picture of the past. These have included Noel Iverson for providing me with information on Nels Anderson's last days, Reba Mathis for her dedication to helping me investigate the life of Paul Cressey, and Jon Snodgrass for some personal insights into Shaw and *The Jack-Roller*.

Finally, a book like this requires support from a host of people and institutions. I'd like to thank Pace University and its scholarly research committee for providing me with some relief from a heavy undergraduate teaching load, so I could focus on this project. Also, I am appreciative of the dean of Pace's School of Arts and Sciences for being supportive in helping to fund my travel to the archives at the University of Chicago and granting me release time when the research committee was financially stretched to its fullest extent. I am also grateful to readers of this manuscript, including Frances Exler, Regina Holmes, Sam Exler and Howard Justin. Most importantly, I'd like to thank my wife, Sandi, for her tireless support and suggestions along the way.

Chapter 1

Sociology Noir and the Chicago School Monographs

THE UNIQUENESS OF AMERICAN SOCIOLOGY is often associated with the development of the Chicago school monographs in the 1920s and 1930s issued under the direction of Robert E. Park, chair of the sociology department at the University of Chicago. The ethnographies dealing with the dark side of urban life, *The Unadjusted Girl*, *The Jack-Roller*, *The Taxi Dance Hall*, *The Gang*, *The Hobo*, and others are reflective of a particular period in the development of an American aesthetic of marginalization characterized by its realistic imagery of outcasts and loners. These works contained revealing treatments of gender, sex, and deviance, and employed many of those elements that were characteristic of pulp fiction and American roman noir.

While many young sociologists who constructed these studies for their graduate theses were no Dashiell Hammetts or Raymond Chandlers, they were influenced by many of the same social forces associated with urban American life during this period. A number of these authors were themselves migrants from rural America living in a big city for the very first time. Many were marginalized and alienated, alone, isolated from friends and relatives. Some were attracted to sociology because of what it sought to understand, others wanted the adventure of exploring the city streets, more were simply fascinated with subjects that were often off-limits to the curious working class individual.

For these Chicago school authors, almost exclusively male, the treatment of gender, sex, and deviance is reflective of a particular period in the history of American scholarship and literature. Their portrayals of prostitutes and thugs, petty criminals and hobos, immigrants and delinquents, helped to move sociology beyond the social gospel discourse of an earlier, moralistic generation. It established a tone of urban naturalism in sociological scholarship that eventually made its way into the American imagination. Their frequent employment of first person narratives, their reliance on diaries and letters, helped to dramatize the feelings of their subjects.

This chapter examines some of the important connections between Chicago school sociology and the noir motif in literature, art, and film.

The Modernist Roots of Noir

Most who encounter the word *noir* in a cultural context associate it with a particular category of American film made in the 1940s and 1950s, shot in black and white and focused on dark city streets and shadowy alleys, cigarette smoke, tough guys, femmes fatales, moral ambiguity, and inordinate violence. But noir is more than this. It is more than film noir—a category, style, or genre of cinema. It is more than the popular hard-boiled pulp detective stories that preceded it or were forever coupled to it and given a noir designation by critics and writers.

Noir emerges from cultures struggling with transition, struggling against traditional constraints and wrestling with the vicissitudes of modern life. Noir is most decidedly urban; it is dominated by men and sometimes women who are in some ways ill fated, or people who survive by being clever but who are frequently disoriented by the currents of modern life. Still, the definition of noir as a dynamic cultural signifier is contentious.

In their seminal work on American film noir, Raymond Borde and Etienne Chaumeton (2002) emphasized its psychological dimensions, mentioning its sociological significance only in passing. For them, noir was a style associated with a "particular sense of malaise" (p.13). Borde and Chaumeton attempted to distinguish film noir as a unique category of cinema. They suggested key elements were central to noir, such as the humanization of criminals, the blurring between good and evil, a sense

6

of pessimism, and the emphasis on erotic violence. For Borde and Chaumeton film noir emerged from a number of social forces set into play by World War II and its aftermath. As a category, it had a short lifespan, disappearing in the 1960s. Today, however, many cultural critics have moved away from this approach. Drawing maps of inclusion and exclusion and determining which criteria most appropriately suit noir's cultural pedigree or history is found to be problematic.

James Naremore (1998) believes that noir transcends borders. For him, noir has become one of the most important intellectual descriptors of recent time. It has many roots and many branches. For Naremore, there is no "right" definition of noir, only an array of uses. He insists that the universal appeal of noir says something about the human condition. While he recognizes the French contribution to the construction of this category, he finds fault in the high culture pedigree that many critics have attached to it.

French film critics, who early on conceptualized the noir style, leaned heavily on psychoanalysis and existentialism to explain its origins and nature. Since these paradigms were extremely popular during the 1940s and 1950s, noir was frequently interpreted through them. Borde and Chaumeton noted that many American hard-boiled fiction writers subscribed to the *Psychoanalytic Review*, implying a causal relationship between theory and product (p. 18). They also implied a direct relationship between high culture, such as surrealism, and film noir (pp. 42–45). While some influences are undeniable, one needs to equally recognize that the American cinematic venture into urban low-life, crime, betrayal, and sex was affected by reading stories in magazines like the *Police Gazette* and sensationalist tabloids that appeared on every city newsstand during that period and even well before it. Letters to the lonely-hearts column of newspapers, police blotter reports, and documentary newsreels on urban crime seem essential to the rise of the noir aesthetic. There was a particular pedestrian essence to these early works in film noir. In fact, Billy Wilder's *Double Indemnity* (1944), with its screenplay by Raymond Chandler, was based on a novella by James M. Cain, who is believed to have based his fiction on the Albert Snyder murder case in Queens County, New York. The murder case involved an adulterous wife who, along with a traveling corset salesman, murdered her husband for insurance money. The story was written up in the tabloid press in 1927. The blurred photograph of the murderess in the electric chair made the front page of the New York *Daily News* and became an icon of ghoulish crime sensationalism (Margolin 1999).

Cain himself had spent much of his younger years as a reporter. While most who read his biography would find it difficult to label him a remote existentialist, the forces that elevated existentialism into popular consciousness also affected the outlook of many artists, writers, and scholars of this era. In this vein it seems both curious and appropriate that Albert Camus would pronounce that reading *The Postman Always Rings Twice* influenced him to write *The Stranger* (Naremore, p. 23).

Cain completed writing *Double Indemnity* in 1935 and submitted it to producer Lawrence Weingarten at MGM that same year. Four other studios, Paramount, Warners, Columbia, and Twentieth Century Fox, had expressed an interest in filming it. But this story, like so many other works that would later become essential to film noir, was rejected by the Hays Commission on the basis of its illicit sexuality and violence (Biesen 2005, p. 99). The commission was to hold back many such stories produced throughout the 1930s.

Marc Vernet (1993, p.14) has posited that there is a most definite "chronological gap" between the artistic source of film noir material and the works' eventual adaptation to the screen. Many stories that were made into film noir screenplays had been written decades before they were made into motion pictures. Like James Naremore, it is Vernet's contention that any attempts to limit this genre to a particular historical epoch are misleading and ignore the fact that noir emerges from a particular modern aesthetic that lives on and transforms itself over time.

The narrow scope of noir aesthetics sees Chandler, Hammett, and Cain anointed by what Jay Hopler (2000) refers to as "snooty gate keeping literati"—those who would not be caught dead reading pulp detective novels and yet have embraced key writers as exemplars of a certain highbrow ethos—and "delightfully cynical American modernists." While elements of noir can be found in the historic currents of both high and low culture, the vast majority of scholars focus on a small elite group but rarely on writers like W.T. Ballard, Dorothy Hughes, Erle Stanley Gardner and others. There certainly appears to be a division between academe's focus on what constitutes the canon in this genre and the thoughts of collectors and fans.

The notion that hard-boiled fiction (often referred to as noir fiction) is a formula consisting of a middle aged white male detective, a femme

Ruth Snyder as she sits in the witness chair in a Queens County court-room on trial for murdering her husband for his life insurance. She was assisted by her lover—a traveling corset salesman. The trial became a tabloid sensation of 1927. The incident was to influence the writing of both *Double Indemnity* (1944) and *The Postman Always Rings Twice* (1946), which were based on stories by James Cain. (Photograph from the New York *Daily News*. Reprinted with permission.)

Sociology Noir

(Copyright: 1928: by Pacific and Atlantic photos)

RUTH SNYDER'S DEATH PICTURED!—This is perhaps the most remarkable exclusive picture in the history of criminology. It shows the actual scene in the Sing Sing death house as the lethal current surged through Ruth Snyder's body at 11:06 last night. Her helmeted head is stiffened in death, her face masked and an electrode strapped to her bare right leg. The autopsy table on which her body was removed is beside her. Judd Gray, mumbling a prayer, followed her down the narrow corridor at 11:14. "Father, forgive them, for they don't know what they are doing?" were Ruth's last words. The picture is the first Sing Sing execution picture and the first of a woman's electrocution. *Story p. 3; other pics, p. 28 and back page.*

Ruth Snyder's electrocution. This New York *Daily News* photograph of January 13, 1928, was to become an important icon of tabloid journalism. (Photograph by Tom Howard for the New York *Daily News*, January 13, 1928. Reprinted with permission.)

fatale, money, a murder, an office, a shadow, a scream, a body, a double-cross, and a twist in plot does not speak to the enormous elasticity of this type of literature. Many critics have argued that such a neat set of elements misses its deeper psychological essence as well as its sociological meaning (Rabinowitz 2002, Naremore 1998, Copjec 1993). According to one author, "Noir is not a kind of Macho Hard-boiled fiction where Tough Guys pass moral judgment on an immoral society. Noir is about the weak-minded, the losers, the bottom feeders..." (Duncan 2000). Paul Duncan makes the point that essential to noir is a quest into a "heart of darkness" (p. 9). While Chicago sociologists certainly would not have used terms like "bottom feeders," many nevertheless were fascinated with those who "lived at the margins." Nicholas Christopher (1997, p. 36), in his remarkable book on film noir and the American city, notes, "Using a simpler, maybe too simple metaphor, we might say that it is a dark mirror, reflecting the dark underside of American urban life—the subterranean city—from which much crime, high and low culture, raw sexual energy, and deviations, and other elemental, ambiguous forces that fuel the greater society often spring."

Noir shall be treated here as a contemporary aesthetic, a popular aesthetic that finds its roots in the working class consciousness. It is a consciousness threatened in its very survival by the machinery of capitalism. It therefore expresses the alienation associated with the subordinated position—one disillusioned by war and nationalism. As an aesthetic it contains an ideology and history of an oppressed class. It constantly calls into question the false opposition of right and wrong promoted by bourgeois society. Essential to its bleakness is an inability to escape, to find an exit, to find a way to a safe place removed from impending doom. Noir is in no way romantic, nor is it revolutionary. It is decidedly critical and reflexive, and makes use of the unconscious.

In some sense, it seems ironic that in order to get to the core of noir one must seek its roots in the high culture of modernism. While in many ways primal, noir, as an aesthetic, is deeply implanted in modernist soil. As a product of modernity, it is neither unified nor uniform. It does, however, conform to many of the characteristics of the modern style (Marling 1994).

As an aesthetic, modernism has been defined (for the most part) by powerful cultural elites who have set limits on the working class role in its construction. Pierre Bourdieu makes this quite clear in his study of

11

the sociology of taste (Bourdieu 1984). Modernism has always recognized the protests against the oppressive aspects of modernity as well as the celebrations of its rewards. What has been historically allowed entry into the dominant culture as modernism must meet stringent aesthetic requirements. Despite its contentious definition in bourgeois circles, many appear to agree on several characteristics inherent in it. Four of these central elements have been noted by Marxist theorist Eugene Lunn (1982, p. 34). First, modernism contains self-reflexiveness or self-consciousness. By this Lunn means that it reveals its own subjectivity. Secondly, it emphasizes simultaneity, juxtaposition, or montage. It is highly metaphoric, often fragmented, and frequently psychological, revealing positions of multiple consciousness. Individual experiences as well as elements of the self are juxtaposed or in conflict. Thirdly, there is paradox here, coupled with ambiguity and uncertainty. And finally, modernism emphasizes a process of dehumanization at work. One can see this in noir violence as well as in its motifs of human objectification and manipulation.

In their essential study of modernism, Malcolm Bradbury and James McFarlane (1976, p. 26) posit that modernism also represents an ongoing disintegration of life as it had been known. To use a classical sociological concept, it represents an ongoing process of social disorganization leading to fear and insecurity:

> Modernism might mean not only a new mode of mannerism in the arts but a certain significant disaster for them. In short, experimentalism does not simply suggest the presence of sophistication, difficulty and novelty in art, it also suggests bleakness, darkness, alienation and disintegration.

There is a consensus that film noir has its roots not only in modernism but also in German expressionism which articulates these modernist sensibilities in a particular way. An analysis of expressionist film, such as that of Robert Wiene, F.W. Murnau or even Fritz Lang and Billy Wilder, reveal these modernist elements most strikingly. All of this art reflects a dark savage world wherein the primal unconscious makes its way into a story. Further evidence of such modernist expressionism can be easily found in the literary work of Franz Kafka, the paintings of Edvard Munch, or the plays of Samuel Beckett and Bertolt Brecht. It is small wonder that Sigmund Freud's focus on the unconscious, on nightmares and dreams, is elevated to a prominent place in bourgeois science and aesthetics.

In fact, Freud's *Interpretation of Dreams*, published in 1900, became an important source of avant garde inspiration. The colorful imagery he later developed of the primitive id and the death instinct, his notion of "everywhere man is a wolf to man," assuredly entered into the realm of European art and social analysis. In the United States it remained quite peripheral until the 1930s and Hitler's rise to power. However, psychoanalysis was integrated into the popular culture just as sociology noir and noir literature were reaching their apex. Of course, it had an influence on how writers, artists, film makers, and sociologists saw the world.

While most locate the origins of modern noir in American hard-boiled fiction and in the World War II American crime cinema that adapted many of these stories to the screen, a large number of noir directors were German émigrés who had witnessed the terrors of World War I and the eventual rise of Nazism. Weimar Germany was the scene of many dark horrors. It had its own detective fiction characterized by deep cynicism and violence. Its press looked at the lecherous side of life—at prostitutes, petty thieves, and sexual murders. These sensibilities of a disillusioned postwar people also made their way into American culture. Émigré directors brought to America a wealth of European sensibilities. Hard-boiled fiction of the 1920s and 1930s was frequently not made into screenplays until the 1940s and 1950s, when these directors had a chance to assimilate into their work the American pragmatic spirit.

Naremore makes the point that French film noir, shadowy melodramas that emerged from the Popular Front in the mid to late 1930s also set the tone for American film noir (p.15). This mélange of American and European influences come together in the development of the noir aesthetic. The assumed descent of noir from high European culture currents must be tempered by historical evidence. While noir resonated with American sentiment of the 1950s, it was in no way exclusively formed by this period in American life.

Artistic, Literary, and Journalistic Foundations

The modernist genealogy of noir might find some of its most basic elements in what historian Mario Praz referred to as "black romanticism," epitomized in the work of Henry Fuseli. Born in Switzerland in 1741, Fuseli had at one time studied to be a priest. He came from a cultured home and was exceedingly well read. His father had been a successful painter. A close friend of William Blake, who wrote of "dark and Satanic mills," Fuseli produced paintings that were rich in symbolism; darkness, shadows, and pending violence reveal an intense sense of dread and anxiety. Much of his work depicts grotesque, almost surreal, dreams. A copy of his most famous painting, *The Nightmare*, hung in Freud's apartment at Berggasse 19, Vienna, in 1926.

Praz discovered in some early romanticism of Fuseli, and others, a sense of "luxurious agonies of delight," an eroticism that embraced cruelty. For Fuseli, violence and death take on elements of the sublime. According to artist B.R. Hayden, in Fuseli's paintings women are always whores driven by hatred, not pleasure; his men are bandits, driven by a "licentious turbulence," rarely by pure desire (Powell 1972, p. 64). It is the position of Borde and Chaumeton, as well as Naremore, that central to most film noir is a dreamlike quality: "Indeed, the narratives themselves are often situated on the margins of dreams, as to intensify the surrealistic atmosphere of violent confusion, ambiguity, or disequilibrium..." (Naremore 1998, p. 21).

As the industrial revolution swept through Europe, an array of modern artists and writers of fiction contributed to the development of the noir sublime. From Delacroix to Goya, bleak landscapes of death and dehumanization came to represent a besieged soul. Wilhelm Dilthey was to note, "It was clear that the eighteenth and nineteenth centuries, being the age of individualism, would bring forth a thoroughly pathological literature in which the individual's endeavors to engender the overall life of humankind, of ideal, became a painful, fatal disease, for the time was not ripe for the ideal to be gasped within life" (Lepenies 1992, p. 59). In American literature, Edgar Allan Poe became the master of combining psychologically oriented detective fiction with macabre suspense.

By the mid-nineteenth century, romanticism (dark and otherwise) had evolved into realism. French authors such as Gustave Flaubert and, later, Charles Baudelaire did much to underscore urban alienation and personal aloneness within the crowd. Baudelaire, in particular, made much of the darkness of city life in his *Les Fleur du mal*. For many mid-nineteenth century writers, including Charles Dickens, cities came to represent darkness of spirit—places void of light and air. Such darkness was associated not only with the deep recesses of the unconscious but also with the blackened factory walls and the rancid smoke which enshrouded the workers.

Dickens, Dostoyevsky, and Conrad, who are often seen as important architects of the modernist noir aesthetic, did much to raise social consciousness of class exploitation and struggled to maintain a sense of humanity in their work (Horsley 2001, p. 19; Duncan 2000, p. 16). Inherent in their writings is a type of inner turmoil fueled by the alienating condition of class relations. For the most part, these are narratives of the oppressed and marginalized. American writers such as Jack London, Upton Sinclair, and Theodore Dreiser would add their voices (Abbott 2002, p. 16).

The sociological content of this work is undeniable. What interests us here is not simply the emphasis of these writers on marginalization and human alienation, which are essential to most hard-boiled fiction. What is key here is the heightened individualistic nature of their protagonists, who make their way through the dark, upside-down world, struggling with issues of moral ambiguity and ambivalence—dealing with matters of conscience in the face of increasing cruelty and human exploitation. While these important writers were in many ways more dissimilar than alike they shared modern sensibilities, which paralleled those expressed by European social philosophers and sociologists of this era. Ferdinand Tönnies, Werner Sombart, and Max Weber, who had laid considerable groundwork for a sociology noir, examined the sense of personal estrangement and nihilism in everyday life (Mitzman 1973; Nisbet 1976). Motifs in their work were quite gloomy. Society was viewed as unraveling and with that unraveling came forms of personal disintegration and melancholia.

Robert Nisbet (1976, p. 115) has noted that these authors shared a close affinity to artists and novelists who surrounded them, picking up almost identical themes in their work (p. 3). While sociology is not fiction (certainly not in its classical sense), Nisbet makes the case that it is a form of art, and it has frequently employed a harsh critique of modernity. He suggests that the notions of an oncoming malaise of the human spirit brought on by the "rust of progress" is inherent in classical sociological work.

While these early works contained many of the antecedents of the noir aesthetic, newspapers were also beginning to play a significant role in the day-to-day lives of people. Both in Europe and the United States there was a meeting of journalism and literature, and struggling writers often found in the penny press a place to ply their trade. In nineteenth century Europe, the press had become a powerful influence on politics and culture. In the United States, rugged individualism appeared to shape more populist sensibilities. This is especially true for popular pulp literature, beginning with story papers and dime novels.

Rolf Lindner (1996) posits that what separated the penny press from its more aristocratic competitors was not its price, but rather its discovery of "the near at hand" (p. 9). For the first time, the abnormal and curious became newsworthy. The penny press invaded the municipal courts, revealing not only tales of human passion and marginalized curiosities but also the life ways of unsavory characters. There is a shadowy richness here that adds to the texture of urban life, which percolates from below.

The German sensationalist press, beginning in Wilhelmine Berlin in the early 1900s, also fed a growing proletarian hunger for tales of violence, thievery, sexual perversion and *lustmord* (Fritzsche 1996; Tartar 1995; Evans 1998). As centers of culture, industry, and revolution, pre-World War I cities offered a stage whereon all manner of social deviance was played out. These occurrences, which happened in these cities' darkest recesses, captured working class imaginations.

In Berlin, the young author and publicist Hans Oswald led a team of university graduates in the creation of what became known as the *Grosstadt-Dokumente*, a series of fifty-one books or pamphlets on the dark and curious side of urban phenomenology. Published between the years 1904 and 1908, each young author focused on a unique aspect of the city's social core—prostitutes, homosexuals, pimps, beggars, vagabonds, department store clerks, and dance hall girls. Oswald himself was a vagabond before devoting himself to this project (Fritzsche 1994). For the most part these writers were not trained sociologists but were affiliated with art circles, social reform organizations and newspapers (Lindner 1996, p. 5). They frequently used governmental reports as well as personal documents such as letters and diaries. Many were known to one another and were participants in Berlin's bohemian cultural life, which also attracted the likes of Georg Simmel, Franz Oppenheimer, and Werner Sombart. Since these works were known to the Chicago school and were purchased by the University of Chicago Library there is considerable evidence of their impact on the thrust of Chicago research, especially on the monographs.

1. Sociology Noir and the Chicago School Monographs

In the United States, dime novels were about 100 pages of narrative with stories that had been serialized in what were then called story papers. These story papers were small newspapers with both fiction and nonfiction pieces ranging from fashion advice to bits of arcane information. While dime novels originated with stories of heroic Western adventures, they later contained stories of human depravity and crime—what were called "mysteries of the city." According to Michael Denning (1987, p. 85), these small and inexpensive novels "unveiled the city's mysteries by telling tales of criminal underworlds, urban squalor, and elite luxury and decadence." With mass distribution and publication in several languages, these books captured the hearts and pocketbooks of the literate urban proletariat.

There can be little doubt that this cheap fiction owed a considerable debt to the penny press and early tabloid journalism. Here stories were often serialized, and gritty street life was revealed in factual police reports. It is Denning's intent in his history of dime novels to reveal the proletarian demeanor of cheap literature by referencing its connection to the working class poor, immigrants, mechanics, shop girls and those who had been marginalized. As the most widely read literature of the nineteenth century, the dime novels and other cheap fiction became central to working class life. Denning sees these first pieces of proletarian fiction as having descended from the penny press and story papers.

The parallel between the proletarian press and cheap fiction in *fin de siecle* Chicago and Wilhelmine Berlin are more than just interesting. They became essential in the development of sociology noir. Court reports of cases involving sexual perversion and degenerative forms of crime are not only raw material for stories in the popular press but also make their way into working class literature for readers both in Berlin and Chicago (Fritzsche 1996). Weimar Berlin was particularly rife with stories of criminals that ran through city newspapers and literature. Like their American counterparts, these pieces tended to humanize the criminal.

Detective and crime stories began to appear in dime novels in the 1870s in the United States. Investigators such as Old Sleuth, Butts, Old Rafferty and the like were examples of proletarian detectives—quite different from Sherlock Holmes of Arthur Conan Doyle or C. August Dupin of Edgar Allan Poe—who were definitively more bourgeois (Denning, p. 148). While some historians point to the influence of the very successful Nick Carter series, an investigator who was well-bred and

17

sophisticated—quite unlike what would come later with hard-boiled fiction, few have closely examined the work of Allan Pinkerton, whose dime novels reveal many of the same elements of later hard-boiled detective fiction: terse prose, a street-wise protagonist "prone to violence," and women "of dubious virtue." It was Pinkerton who settled in Chicago and opened the very first private detective agency there. It was from those experiences that his stories emerged.

Many consumers of dime novels eagerly read the weekly penny press—newspapers filled with sensational accounts of local crime and personal disaster. Many who wrote for these newspapers also wrote cheap fiction (Denning 1988). *The Sun, The Morning Herald,* and *The New World* circulated from local newsstands. These city tabloids gained increasingly larger circulations as the nineteenth century came to a close. With increasing circulation, publication became more frequent. Some tabloids published more than one daily edition. Scandalous accounts of murders, rapes and gang violence, which appeared in the penny press, made their way into the material of dime novels. By the late eighteen hundreds, reporters were accompanying police on raids of brothels, opium dens, and back room illicit gambling ventures. They sat in courtrooms as observers and their work often informed cheap fiction.

These tabloid-inspired stories were sensationalistic accounts of the lives of real people, members of the *Lumpenproletariat.* The penny press carried tales of shootings, robberies, and white slavery immigrant exploitation, as well as barroom brawls. Many of these stories were voyeuristic travels onto the meanest streets, which were quiet by day but alive at night. The stories often examined gang violence, domestic assaults and ax murders. The reader would vicariously follow the journalist into a dingy tenement to witness hungry children living in rat-infested squalor. They'd read about the corruption of city officials and the crimes of businessmen. As the journalists got too close to issues of class domination, there was a strong establishment reaction.

This was also true for early American cinema. Kevin Brownlow (1990), in his study of social conscience in silent film, provides ample evidence that the power of movies to illuminate contemporary social ills was enormous. In fact, nickelodeons, which overwhelmingly appealed to urban working class audiences, were often viewed as breeding grounds for sedition (p. xvi). By 1910 twenty-six million people frequented silent theatres each week, and often viewed work that dealt with urban sociological themes. "The early social films often contained precious histori-cal evidence," noted Brownlow. "Some were shot in the slum districts and big cities; others featured the very people at the center of contro-versy (p. xxi)." Brownlow asserts that it was the Hays Act that helped put an end to these socially conscious films. Many of the earliest silent films contained elements of crime, prostitution, poverty, and juvenile delin-quency. And some even featured detectives. Filmmakers, some of whom had been writers and journalists, peered into the darkest caverns of the city.

Early German cinema as well as the popular press focused on the darkness and violence of the underworld (Evans 1998; Phal 1991). Joe May, an Austrian film director and producer, was central to early German silent cinema. After studying in Berlin, he began making films there in 1912. By 1914 he had embarked on producing a series of successful detec-tive films. It was May who helped bring Fritz Lang into the motion pic-ture business in 1914. And while working with the most important German film studio of that time, Ufa, he had a significant impact on the creation of expressionist film (Redaktion and Lenssen 1991). Later, Weimar cinematography contained many of the essential visual elements that became integral to film noir. German filmmaking evolved as a major influence on American motion pictures, especially crime films. Fritz Lang's M focused on criminals, serial child murder, and the underclass. This story was taken from the German press. Lang would later leave Nazi Germany to make some of the most important American noir classics.

The early attacks against both the penny press, cheap fiction, and pedestrian realism in cinema appear to reflect a true class division in society. Much of the writings directed toward the proletarian reader and filmgoer might have contained an excess of sex, blood and melodrama, but a good bit of it also challenged the status quo. The need to control the poor through "better" and "more appropriate" literature had been an important bourgeois issue as early as the late 1800s. And Denning gives evidence that many of the anti-vice organizations that sprung into action to launch these attacks were populated by the societal elites who had an interest in quieting the so-called rabble. Newspapers founded in the lat-ter part of the nineteenth century contained human-interest stories, crime stories, and tales of corporate abuse. The press became increasingly soci-ological in its focus. All of this made its way into early film.

Many social reformers invaded the third estate, and others the cinema. Some writers became reformers after working for newspapers. Lincoln Stephens, Upton Sinclair, and Jacob Riis uncovered the social crimes of cities while working as journalists for newspapers. The new journalism, which was a movement away from control of the press by partisan political parties and the emergence of a commercial press offering both entertainment and information, allowed independent writers a place to eke out a living. It also enabled workers to gain a sense of connection to the urban world in which they lived. It was here, writing for the penny press, where many intellectuals, poets and novelists got their start. Often, the so-called new journalists were writing to keep a roof over their heads. Early reporters often carried a reputation as heavy drinkers living in a world of night, sleeping by day. Many identified themselves with American bohemianism. They often saw themselves as outcasts and counter-culture types, and frequently associated with other outcasts: artists, actors, and intellectuals. Many were socialists and others free love advocates, some were supporters of women's suffrage or were suffragettes themselves, and some were homosexuals or defenders of homosexuality. Some writers, such as George Gissing, already lived on the margins of society. Carl Sandburg, Sherwood Anderson, Theodore Dreiser, Edgar Lee Masters, and Upton Sinclair at one time survived by writing for the penny press. Eugene Debs, W.E.B. DuBois and even Karl Marx attempted to support themselves as journalists.

It is where the penny press and story papers meet the dime novel that intrigues us. It is here where stories from police reports and court transcripts jump from the pages of proletarian newspapers and make their way into cheap fiction. Such fiction becomes central to the city dweller's life. This interplay of fact and fancy is essential to the thrust of this investigation. It is here where we find the origins of a newly emerging American sociology, which is itself sensationalistic and to some extent quite literary.

Journalism, Literature, and Sociology Noir

Sociology noir emerged from a host of social forces associated with urbanization and modernization. It was a response to those same conditions that worked to produce tabloid journalism and cheap fiction. The eclipse of communal living, the rapid growth of industrial cities, the rise

A blind street vendor of balloons (George John) identified Hans Beckert (Peter Lorre) as the elusive child molester in Fritz Lang's M (1931). An important example of German Expressionism, its style was emulated in American film noir.

of a literate working class coupled with enormous waves of migrants and immigrants and associated anomie helped not only to spur the emergence of the popular press and cheap fiction, but also laid the groundwork for new urban research and scholarship in academia.

In fact, in the United States, sociology noir frequently imitated the tabloid journalists' investigations into flophouses, immigrant workers, taxi dance halls, juvenile delinquency, criminal gangs, and the lives of tramps and prostitutes. It looked at the underbelly of urban life, at the subterranean city and the marginalized people who inhabited it. It examined domestic disputes, sexual infidelity, and a host of other modern phenomena. Its audience, however, was quite different from factory workers, shop girls and low level office clerks who eagerly awaited the evening edition of the paper and tended to be more educated and middle class.

Sociology noir's methods, too, sought a higher ground. Stories that emerged from the popular press were converted into objects of scientific investigation inclusive of data collection, charts and graphs. Sensationalism was sanitized. Still, many investigations of urban street life conducted by Chicago students and faculty became the subject of journalistic exposés (Lindner 1996).

Sociology noir was driven by its subject matter, not by a sophisticated methodology or set of complex theories. Part of its attraction was that its method did not get in the way of the narrative. For the most part it was descriptive. While it was sometimes considered a crude product of scholarly researchers, it was appealing in that it told stories that often read like fiction. Clifford Shaw, who wrote of street punks and jack-rollers, would have been right at home with fellow Chicagoans and pulp writers like Vincent Starrett or Craig Rice who contributed to *True Detective Tales*, which was a publication based in that city. The same might be said of Paul Cressey and Harvey Zorbaugh, whose works on taxi dancers and slum dwellers, respectively, shared commonalities with noir fiction of this era.

While this form of narrative sociology was neither exclusive to the United States nor to the University of Chicago, it did give Robert Park and his department international renown. Prior to coming to the university, Park was a tabloid journalist as well as a man of letters. He had tried his hand at serious fiction and poetry; this is all reflected in his own creative and innovative style. As a research supervisor he demanded that his students never lose sight of the humanity of people they were studying. While social processes interested him greatly, he was far more moved by the human quality of his subjects. He was deeply informed by literature and attracted to an American bohemianism that was reexamining if not overtly challenging the social mores of the day. His wife was an artist; his biographer suggests that Park was himself part of this new bohemianism (Raushenbush 1979). His colleague, W.I. Thomas, was also a man of letters who had served as a professor of literature at Oberlin College where he taught the classics before coming to the University of Chicago to complete his doctorate in sociology in 1896.

Not far from the University of Chicago campus, in fact within walking distance, was one of the oldest bohemian sections of the city—the Jackson Park Colony. Situated near the Lake along 57th Street and Stoney Island Avenue in temporary housing that was constructed for concessionaires of the Chicago World's Fair, writers and painters converted these commercial facilities into studios and residences. Often both students and faculty from the sociology department congregated there in the summers to mix with Carl Sandburg, Sherwood Anderson, and others (Carey 1975, p. 181). Although this writers' colony disappeared in the late 1920s, it was not unusual for the artistic and intellectual community to gather there. Vincent Starrett, who eventually made his living writing hard-boiled fiction, became part of the community (Starrett 1965, p. 173). Such places were incubators of radical social thought.

While Park received much of the credit by historians for the work of the Chicago school, it was Thomas who was central to the ethnographic approach for which that school became famous. Furthermore, it was Thomas who imbued this new sociology with theory grounded in German subjectivist philosophy that had also influenced his work as a literary scholar and critic. It was Professor Thomas who recommended Park for a position at Chicago. While Park was a much more pragmatic academic, Thomas was a scholar who went on to deeply and directly influence the course of social interactionist theory.

Both of these men were remarkably different from the generation of sociologists that preceded them at the University of Chicago. That generation was primarily comprised of clergy, some more secular than others, but nonetheless men trained as ministers and connected to social gospel. Albion Small, who first hired Thomas and later Park, saw sociology as mainly a Christian endeavor. Park and Thomas expended great effort to distance their sociology from that of the department's founders.

In many ways Thomas and Park were iconoclasts. While they had emerged from nonurban backgrounds (Thomas from the South and Park from the Midwest), they were in tune with the social changes taking place around them. Both Thomas and Park had studied in Germany as graduate students and spent significant time in Berlin, intrigued by the city's *fin de siècle* culture. Thomas was there in 1889 and Park in 1899 (Janowitz 1966, p. xii; Matthews 1977, p. 34). Both were influenced by German folk psychology but were also fascinated by the type of avant gardism found there in the arts.

Park was drawn to Georg Simmel, who showed how popular culture could become a serious subject of investigation. Berlin's newspapers also influenced Park, who had begun writing about the press for his dissertation but eventually turned to a comprehensive study of the crowd. The crowd as well as newspapers were important leitmotifs in German scholarship. The revelry and beauty of the Berlin Alexanderplatz exerted an influence on writers and artists from all walks of life. In fact, there is considerable evidence that Park's interest in urban ethnography and the underbelly of city life was influenced by the German press and what was to emerge as the *Grosstadt-Dokumente*, which dealt with the dark phenomenology of life in Berlin (Jazbinsek, Joerges and Thies 2001). These works would come to influence his own writings, and would be a model for the work of many of his students. According to historian Peter Fritzsche (1994), the *Grosstadt-Dokumente* did much of what the Chicago school would become renowned for, and even projected the city as an ecological system. Later, Park would describe Chicago in the same fashion (pp. 389–390).

A sketch of Robert E. Park done by his wife, Clare Cahill, in Berlin in 1900. Leader of the Chicago School, Park was much influenced by his studies in Germany. (Photograph reprinted with permission from the Special Collections Research Center, University of Chicago Library.)

Park's arrival at the University of Chicago marked a turning point for sociology there. However, Thomas had already laid much of the groundwork in opening up the study of urban society. He moved his students further away from rigid moralisms of the previous generation. Thomas himself had done groundbreaking work on the lives of Polish immigrants in Chicago. Along with Florian Znaniecki he integrated anthropological methodology into his study by using personal diaries and letters. This study was far removed from the quantitative studies being conducted at other American universities where sociology was being taught. It was also very different from the massive population surveys that had earlier been conducted by social demographers. It was more personal and emotional, and emphasized the sense of human alienation and aloneness that appeared characteristic of urban life. This was an interest and orientation he shared with Robert Park.

Park had written extensively on marginality—the marginality of immigrants, blacks, and the poor. Through his graduate students, Park explored the underbelly of urban life. Human-interest stories became the subjects of graduate theses. Sexual mores, which had been off-limits, became legitimate avenues of investigation. Where at one time the faculty had taken strong moralistic positions regarding family and cultural life, the younger and more secular members began to see things in more relativistic terms. Certainly, some of the work of younger scholars maintained elements of Park's personal notion of social breakdown and disorganization. Park shared with Jane Addams and other progressives a belief in Americanization of the immigrant and the need for assimilation. But this notion stood in opposition to his heartfelt position that sociologists needed to be nonjudgmental and shy away from proscribing measures to ensure conformity. For the most part, his work was a celebration of otherness. He did not believe sociologists should judge others.

Sexual mores and the role of women were undergoing enormous change in the early 1900s. Thomas and his wife, Harriet Park, had been very active in the suffrage movement, and Thomas had written extensively on the subject of sexuality. While not a remarkable piece of research, *The Unadjusted Girl* shed light on the changing conditions affecting women at this time in the city of the post–World War I era. Moral ambiguity, homosexuality, sexual infidelity and prostitution revealed much about American society and Thomas understood this. He used letters from lonely-hearts columns to illustrate his points. The Victorian era was coming to an end. In a sense, Thomas celebrated this. Also, he emphasized the cultural and moral relativism that surrounded him. Immigrants brought with them different ways of living. Racial tensions were increasing and so was crime. The students and faculty at Chicago were enthralled by the cultural diversity and excitement of urban life.

It is not in the least bit remarkable that some of the most important literary figures to emerge in Chicago in the 1920s and 1930s would have come through the sociology department at the University of Chicago and would frequently draw upon their studies in sociology. Carla Capetti (1993) has done an outstanding job describing this relationship between Chicago school sociology and the work of Richard Wright, James T. Farrell, Nelson Algren, and others. Capetti sees Chicago school sociology as married to a literary tradition, a tradition of urban writers dealing with issues of class, race, violence, crime and personal estrangement. (Her thesis will be explored further in chapter two.) But this tradition also can be seen as related to noir fiction, since many of these authors' works have a particular affinity to the hard-boiled style.

While Chicago does not hold a major claim to hard-boiled fiction as it emerged in Mencken's *Black Mask* in the 1920s and 1930s, it was the birth place of Raymond Chandler and a host of other hard-boiled writers and pulp publications, including Clyde B. Clason and *True Detective Magazine*. In the 1920s the city was becoming an American crime capital; as such, Chicago offered much more than New York or Los Angeles in the way of mapping criminality. It appears inconceivable that the early monographs, those early ethnographies on thieves and prostitutes, would have been written anywhere else. Writing on hard-boiled crime fiction of this era, Sean McCann (2000) draws a connection between the Chicago school and the work of noir author Caroll John Daly, one of the most successful pulp writers of the day. McCann notes that both Thomas and Park "saw the city in terms close to those that ran through *Black Mask* at that time" (p. 128). While McCann does not explore these connections in detail, he does welcome such analysis.

Sociology noir emerged in the dark city of Chicago as a result of a confluence of social forces. These forces helped give rise to noir fiction as well. New journalism, noir literature, and urban sociology all reached down into the dark recesses of city life to capture a picture of the tormented human psyche—the marginalized, the lonely, the ambivalent. It portrayed the moral uncertainty of this era, an era where many were still reeling from the horrors of World War I.

Robert E. Park captured the essence of this shift in American urban life by directing his students to find humanity in places most scholars would overlook—in the dance halls, pool rooms, flophouses, and hobo flats of the day. These scholars would not just present statistical information, but would collect personal stories—first person narratives common to the lives of marginalized peoples.

Park understood the power of these narratives. He became a promoter of a new form of urban research that found an audience in sympathetic bourgeois readers. The University of Chicago Press churned out over a dozen of these monographs dealing with the noir of urban life. These works were reviewed in the popular press and many went into several printings. The sociology department at Chicago gained a reputation as a center of ethnographic work. As Carlo Rotella (1998) noted in his study of urban literature, "The field observers of the Chicago School practiced a kind of theoretically informed anecdotal reportage, making for a markedly journalistic and even novelistic brand of social science" (p. 51). The 1940s and 1950s marked the high point of Chicago school popularity. This corresponded directly with the ascent of film noir. Post World War II saw an even greater emphasis in the arts on disillusionment and social anomie. However, by the 1960s interest in this type of scholarship was beginning to wane. Major cultural revolutions refocused attention on structural shifts, sparking a renewed interest in functionalism and in theories of social conflict.

But it would be inaccurate to write off sociology noir as a product of a specific time, or to see it as having disappeared with a simple paradigm shift. Its great popularity at a particular point in American history, however, did resonate with the fashion of the day. In the same sense, similar things have been said of film noir. Naremore goes to great lengths to show that noir as a style remains deeply embedded in the culture of modernity. Just as noir elements continue to be found in motion pictures, often referred to as neo-noir, sociology has never been fully separated from this venture into the shadowy mean streets. While the University of Chicago might have been the heart of production of early sociology noir, the work of William Foote Whyte, schooled at Chicago, and Elliot Liebow continued in this tradition. Philippe Bourgois, Martin Sanchez-Jankowski and Donna Gaines carry on in the noir vein today and have been joined by a host of younger, innovative scholars in both sociology and cultural anthropology who have taken to the streets. Noir lives on in these works.

Conclusion

The emergence of sociology noir in the 1920s and 1930s can be seen as having been affected by social forces that emerged at the time. These included the rise of popular journalism, film, and fiction and the focus on the marginalized individual who stood outside the established order of things. It was influenced by strong cultural currents of modernism that emphasized the decay of traditional values, including the disintegration of a moral order frequently dealt with by modern novelists such as Dostoyevsky and Conrad. It emerged from the blood and carnage of World War I, the U.S. Prohibition Act of 1920, and the rise of organized crime.

Sociology noir, like hard-boiled fiction and film noir, was one set of interpretations of political and social currents of the day. It was deeply embedded in the ethos of urbanism and American pragmatism, but found an affinity to European aesthetics, ranging from expressionism to psychoanalysis. Its focus on the *other*, the marginalized, the deviant, avoided larger political questions and issues.

While it cannot be argued that this urban sociology was a type of literature, it can be easily posited that it was part of a larger noir narrative emerging from the forces of modernity that encompassed art, literature, and film—work that had the city at its core and which focused on loneliness, alienation, and social marginality. It is in this work that personal life at the margins becomes a central sociological concern.

Chapter 2

W.I. Thomas and Robert E. Park: Chicago Noir

A S THE NINETEENTH CENTURY CAME to a close, the city of Chicago seemed to consume masses of unskilled workers who poured into it from the adjacent farmlands and foreign countries. The concentration of people into inadequate housing exerted pressure on existing facilities and services. Between 1880 and 1890, the population of the city increased by over 100 percent, establishing Chicago as the second largest city in the United States. The city was environmentally unhealthy, unattractive, and a dangerous place in which to reside. The Great Fire of 1871 and another in 1874 devastated an already traumatized populace, tortured the landscape, and left 100,000 people homeless (Johnson and Sautter 1994, p. 27).

Along with the Columbian Exposition, or Chicago World's Fair of 1893, which attempted to beautify and rehabilitate a distressed metropolis, the University of Chicago rose out of the smoldering urban ashes. A massive bequest from John D. Rockefeller allowed the American Baptist Education Society to open the university in the shadow of the newly erected Ferris wheel at the Midway in 1892.

The American Midwest was ripe for a world-class institution of higher education. Certainly many writers and poets had gathered in Chicago. Sherwood Anderson, Theodore Dreiser, and Carl Sandburg had already become nationally renowned figures in the arts. The Art Institute, established in 1879, and the Chicago Symphony Orchestra that was founded in 1891 had begun making the city an important cultural center. And with the recruitment of prominent scholars from around the nation, the University of Chicago was woven into the vibrant fabric of the growing city.

The university's architect, Henry Ives Cobb, modeled its buildings on the English Gothic design of Oxford University. Just like architecture of Daniel Burnham, this work attempted to bring a sense of history and culture to a place that had almost none, a place made raw by physical devastation. But despite the spurt of new building, including the new Art Institute, the city remained both physically and socially distressed for some time.

William Rainey Harper, a Baptist minister and veteran of social gospel who had been recruited from Yale, assumed the university's first presidency and almost immediately secured for the institution an important place in higher education, with a special claim on Christian urban reform. Alongside Jane Addams' Hull House and other civic and religious progressive institutions, Harper saw the university as an instrument that could be used to redress the human desolation created by the industrial machine (Goodspeed 1928).

The same year that the university opened its doors, Harper hired Albion W. Small to oversee the division of social sciences and to develop and chair a department of sociology. Small, who left a position as president of Colby College, asserted that the mandate of sociology was ultimately Christian. The son of a Baptist minister and a former ministerial student himself, he had pursued graduate studies in Berlin and Leipzig with such renowned sociologists as Adolph Wagner and Gustav von Schmoller. After receiving his doctorate in welfare economics from Johns Hopkins, he set to work adapting many of the strategies learned from his German teachers to both the study of cities and the construction of programs of social amelioration (Christakes 1978).

While Small did not contribute a great deal to the scholarship of sociology, he was responsible for putting together a department that would gain international acclaim. Along with Charles Henderson, his collaborator on a number of projects, he focused on issues of ethical and societal reform. Nearly the entire department was comprised of clergymen or sons of clergymen at this time. Often the sociology department was working closely with the divinity school (Smith 1988).

The university in general and the department in particular struggled with its identity—pulled between seeing itself as a bastion of scientific investigation on one hand and an instrument of Christian service on the other. Harper, Small, and Henderson joined forces with local businessmen, journalists, clergy, and social reformers to address the problems of one of the most important world cities—a city that represented a new generation of urban places quite different from its European or American counterparts. It was a city that symbolized modernity in all of its manifestations, both positively and negatively. The strong Christian sentiment would not disappear from sociology until the arrival of W.I. Thomas and Robert E. Park.

This chapter examines how Thomas and Park came together to help construct a particularly American brand of social science. While chapter three deals in greater detail with Thomas's own work, it is important to provide some historical background to his role in the development of the Chicago school itself and his role in helping to establish the urban noir aesthetic. The simultaneous emergence of hard-boiled fiction is seen not merely as coincidental to but as the result of cultural currents that affected both modern sociology and literature.

W.I. Thomas and Subjective Understanding

If there was ever a central figure that moved Chicago away from its religiously oriented social reform path and more toward a secular and scholarly one it was William I. Thomas. Thomas had come to Chicago to study for his doctorate in sociology after a long and distinguished teaching career in the field of literature at Oberlin College. He already held a Ph.D. in the classics from the University of Tennessee before commencing his studies in sociology at Chicago in 1893.

A product of the rural South, Thomas had also studied in Germany and was intrigued by the work of Moritz Lazarus and Heymann Steinthal and the idea of folk psychology. Here was a study that connected the development of culture to the development of personal understanding of the world. It was from these studies that his ethnographic approach was developed. He brought back with him a unique perspective on cities, one considerably less moralistic than any of his teachers.

A brilliant student of Small, Thomas was asked to teach several courses and was eventually appointed to a full-time position in sociology in 1895, becoming a full professor in 1910. It was Thomas who was greatly impressed by the work of a former city journalist, Robert E. Park. Park worked for nearly ten years as a police reporter in Chicago, St. Louis, and New York before going on to do his graduate work in Germany and coming under the influence of Georg Simmel there. His dissertation was on crowds and urban marginalization.

Both Thomas and Park shared a strong interest in issues of race and race relations. They met at a conference in Tuskegee in 1912. At the urging of Thomas, Park joined the sociology faculty at Chicago in 1914.

W.I. Thomas must be credited with opening up an avenue of research that Robert Park would later pursue. Thomas's interest in ethnographic research came from his own reading of Franz Boas and his German experience. In Germany, ethnographic study had already made its way into academic anthropology, psychology, and sociology.

In the beginning, anthropology fared rather poorly at Chicago. While Harper had hired an anthropologist, Frederick Starr, to teach in his social science division, he assigned him to Small's department where he shared space with sociologists and little else. Starr had only an honorary doctorate and came from a geology background. In large part, he was selected for the post as a result of his past association with Harper. His interests were digs and archeological artifacts. He had more in common with the natural scientists than the social scientists and added nothing to the ethnographic flavor of the Chicago school (Bulmer 1984, pp. 39–40). While he was considered a fine lecturer, he was often away working on archeological excavations in remote places and not available to his students.

Thomas's emphasis on ethnography was to become the hallmark of Chicago school sociology. It had not been a method favored by Small. Park himself made little use of it although he valued its applicability. Whereas Park preferred to put a more structural spin on his work, which was grounded in ecological models and empirical research, Thomas leaned toward subjective, biographical renditions of the lives of city people. Where their work merged was in their mutual interest in the subject of urban marginality—in the immigrants, tramps, prostitutes, and petty thieves. These lives represented the textual richness of the city.

Thomas was fascinated with human sexuality and the changes taking place in sexual attitudes. Also, he had a very strong interest in the role of women in society and was politically involved in the suffrage move-ment. He worked closely with Jane Addams at Hull House. It was through her work that Thomas became familiar with the problems encountered by newly arriving immigrants (Deegan 1986, pp. 121–132). His published work with Florian Znaniecki, *The Polish Peasant in Europe and America (1918-1919),* was a superior piece of scholarship that utilized the tools of a social ethnographer and established research standards that others would emulate. In 1939, Robert Park would write: "It is in the work of W.I. Thomas, I believe, that the present tradition of research at Chicago was established" (quoted in Kurtz, 1984, p. 3).

Robert E. Park and the City

When Robert Park came to teach at Chicago, he was fifty years old and already had a career as a journalist and assistant to Booker T. Wash-ington. Whereas Thomas was a child of the South, Park was born in Pennsylvania and raised in the Midwest. However, as an adult, he spent a considerable amount of time in the South working for Washington. Before this he traveled extensively writing for newspapers and magazines.

His life as a reporter opened his eyes to things he would have not seen had he remained at home in Red Wing, Minnesota, running his father's business. He entered journalism at a time when newspapers began reaching out to a wide body of readers with stories of human interest. Park seemed to enjoy the din of seedy urban life. This served him well when he came to teach in Chicago (Matthews 1977, pp. 8–11).

A true cosmopolitan, Park identified with the liberal views of Thomas. Both men (now middle aged) seemed to be struggling with relin-quishing their own conservative upbringing and challenging the reac-tionary ideologies of their time. When Park was brought into the university to teach part time in 1913, he and Thomas were already good friends. "Gradually," noted Fred Matthews, his biographer, "on his own initiative, Park worked his way into a key position in the Chicago Depart-ment" (Matthews 1977, p. 85). Where Thomas was a flamboyant public intellectual and often considered radical in his manner and beliefs, Park was more in tune with the staid character of the university administra-tion. He attended church services regularly and shared a similar Christ-ian orientation toward sociology. Yet he remained ambivalent about the connection between science and religion. Both he and Small shared a similar ambivalence toward do-gooders. Park was in no way a reclusive academic. Like Thomas, he enjoyed roaming the city streets, finding excitement and personal energy there.

Small, Thomas, and Park became the central figures of what is often referred to as the first generation of the Chicago school. It was important for Park to establish for himself a role in the departmental effort to promote a new course of urban research among their students. While his success wasn't immediate, he was able to pull together a variety of resources that could be put to use in developing a new research agenda that could support both student efforts and the reputation of the university in the community. This had been the goal of Small all along. Small and Charles Henderson worked to develop ties with the Chicago School of Civics and Philanthropy, where some of the very first field studies of immigrants were conducted by activists such as Edith Abbott and Sophonisba Breckenridge. Small believed that such research needed to be placed under one roof.

Robert Park saw a need to move these studies into a more scientifically oriented direction and to place them under academic supervision. The Chicago School of Civics and Philanthropy became the University's School of Social Service Administration in 1920. Park had little interest in connecting these studies to the social reform movement, which had been a goal of Small, Henderson, and other civic leaders.

In 1915 Charles Henderson died and in 1916 W.I. Thomas was dismissed from the university under a cloud of sexual scandal and controversy. That same year a young Ernest Burgess, who had studied with Thomas and Small and received his doctorate in sociology from Chicago, was hired as an assistant professor. Burgess's father was a minister in the Congregational church in Oklahoma.

In 1919 Robert Park was appointed to a full-time position in the department to fill a gaping void. He immediately gained the confidence and support of Albion Small, who seemed to have been morally defeated with Thomas's dismissal. Small appeared to grant Park free rein in shaping the future of the program.

Park's entrepreneurial and managerial skills enabled him to develop the department as an effective mechanism for producing scholarly research that would bring renown to the University. He capitalized on Small's and Henderson's associations with charity agencies throughout the city and found in these organizations placements for students that would defray the costs of their research. Drawing upon his experience as a city journalist, he set up a system of assignments, identifying potential "stories" for students to cover. He developed excellent relations with key faculty throughout the university, including Charles Merriam in political science, and helped to organize the Local Community Research Committee (LCRC) through which considerable Rockefeller Foundation money flowed (Bulmer 1984, pp. 138–139). Park and Burgess worked closely together on a variety of research projects.

Chicago had become a cauldron of social unrest. It had a long history of bloody strikes and labor rebellions, but in 1919 it experienced one of the most violent racial upheavals in American history. Money directed to the university was not merely subsidizing research; the sponsors wanted to see practical results. Park had become an extremely influential figure at the university and gained a national reputation as a specialist in race relations. His abilities to secure funding and to direct it toward productive studies were widely recognized (Matthews 1977, pp. 111–113).

In 1923 the department began to receive substantial funding from the Laura Spellman Rockefeller Memorial Fund through the LCRC. The newly established National Social Science Research Council also started to provide substantial grants to underwrite research of the sociologists at the university. Often the big foundations funneled money through the university to support projects conducted at local welfare agencies in Chicago by graduate students, under the supervision of faculty.

With funding mechanisms in place Park looked for a publication outlet for the work. The University of Chicago Press, which had been founded by President Harper, was the logical venue. The press had already been successfully publishing the works of faculty and graduate students— both monographs and journal articles. *The American Journal of Sociology*, published by the press, had already gained an international reputation. Rockefeller money was funneled to the press through the LCRC.

By the early 1920s, The University of Chicago Press had become the outlet for a series of sociological monographs that would deal with the seamy side of city life. Park's aspirations as a journalist and writer seemed to find some degree of fulfillment in this venture. He supervised or wrote introductions to a series of important books written by graduate students. The monographs, which were products of both research and imagination, found acceptance in the literary world of Chicago. They were reviewed in the same magazines and newspapers as the fictionalized accounts of the shadowy side of urban life. It appeared as though Park and his venture into the sociology of urban marginality found a niche somewhere between muckraking journalism and American naturalist literature.

Hard-boiled Fiction and Vice City

The city of Chicago could not have been a better venue for the launching of an American sociology noir. Many urban writers of fiction had already begun to grapple with the issues people confronted living in modern industrial cities. While not all of this fiction can be considered noir, or even hard-boiled, it was influenced by the same social currents that affected young sociologists of this era.

For the most part urban abuses took place in the shadows. People seemed to be affected by the intensity of the struggle to survive. In the city, said Louis Wirth (Park's favorite student), people are almost never neighbors; they find it difficult to determine their own best interest, they become detached, alone in the crowd. He noted: "Frequent close physical contact, coupled with great social distance, accentuates the reserve of unattached individuals toward one another and, unless compensated by other opportunities for response, gives rise to loneliness" (Wirth 1938, p. 9). He went on to note that bitter strife underlying urban life stems from the operation of the "pecuniary nexus," or cutthroat capitalism, which leads to "predatory relationships."

Many of these images are found in the fiction of the day. Certainly, by the 1920s, Chicago had already become an American crime capital. Prostitution and gambling were ingrained in its fabric. This was a "hub city" through which businessmen moved across the country to score a deal; sometimes they settled and stayed. The town had its nightclubs or cabarets, its "resorts," its flophouses, and its hobohemia. The city was infected by governmental corruption, pummeled by racial and ethnic discord, and shaken by labor unrest. In the early 1900s Chicago was a city seething with social and political strife.

When the term "hard-boiled" is applied to fiction, it speaks of characters beaten down by these failings of urban life who nevertheless come to terms with the vicissitudes of the city; these are people who have come to know their way around. It takes a shrewd, cunning, and outwardly callous individual who is wise to the ways of the streets to maneuver safely through the urban labyrinth. Chicago was not the place for highbrow bourgeois investigators who were afraid to dirty their hands. This was a city of slaughterhouses, stockyards, and meatpacking plants whose streets were already stained with blood. Pulp fiction grew up easily in Chicago and found a home there. That Allan Pinkerton, the first American private eye, set up shop in this city in the mid–1800s is no surprise. His dime novels and short stories were the first to celebrate the adventures of the dirty business in which he was engaged. Dashiell Hammett, who never lived in Chicago, would later work as a Pinkerton operative for a number of years, first in Baltimore and then traveling around the country collecting his own stories from his detective experiences to be used in his fiction.

In 1922 and 1923, the very same years that W.I. Thomas was working on his important study, *The Unadjusted Girl, Black Mask* published the first detective fiction of Dashiell Hammett and Carroll John Daly. *Black Mask* became the first pulp magazine devoted to hard-boiled fiction. As the story is told, the magazine was founded by H.L. Mencken and George Jean Nathan as a means of keeping their literary magazine, *Smart Set*, financially afloat. Pulp fiction had a proletarian popularity that was lacking in the "*beau ideal.*" The 1920s and World War I had changed the face of American culture and its demographic landscape. Americans had become more urban, cynical, literate, sexual, and paranoid; their tastes were more diverse. Literature in its infinite variety was reflecting many of these facets of city life. Pulp fiction in its varied forms—western, romance, adventure, and mystery, had displaced the dime novel in serving working-class tastes. According to Frank Krutnik, in his study of this phenomenon, "From the 1920s to the 1950s, the pulps were, like the movies themselves, among the most prominent vehicles for popular fiction" (p. 34). In fact, by 1934 about one hundred fifty pulp magazines could be found on the nation's newsstands (Nevins 1988, p. 125).

Carroll John Daly is considered to be the first hard-boiled fiction writer. It was his stories, not Hammett's, that set the tone for much investigative pulp fiction that dominated the years between the wars. "The False Burton Combs," published by Daly in December of 1922, is considered by many to be *Black Mask's* first venture into this genre and a prototype for hard-boiled fiction (Horsley, p. 27). Here, Daly has a first-person narrator tough guy who speaks in colloquial English and uses humor, wisecracks and sarcasm as weapons, resorting to his gun only when required by circumstance, which is often enough. Daly's fallible protagonist occupies a shadowy space between the police and the world of crime. It is this space that sets the hard-boiled protagonist apart from the heroic detectives of the past. In a sense, it is this focus on marginality and those who dwell in this marginalized space that is so characteristic of the Chicago school sociology. The territory occupied by Daly's characters is not ideal. But it seems very real. The language of the street is central to Daly's unnamed narrator, as it is to those who become subjects of the Chicago school field interviews. And it is the ability of the reader to identify with these voices, or at least recognize them as familiar ones, that gives his stories enormous appeal.

It was Dashiell Hammett who used his talent to make hard-boiled fiction more literary and significantly more appealing to the middle classes. Hammett's work resonated with a more sophisticated audience, despite the fact that Daly remained more popular into the late 1940s. Hammett's work bore the mark of a social critic sensitive to the corrupting influences of American capitalism, yet deeply cynical.

Personal intimidation and sexual manipulation came to represent processes evident in capitalistic society. Greed, corruption, alienation, and moral ambivalence were central elements of both hard-boiled fiction and the ethnographic sociology that grew out of the postwar period.

In the 1920s, Chicago was an arena of vice and corruption while maintaining a proud history of socialist radicalism. Gangs rose up to take violent control over areas of the city; the underworld established its headquarters here. Criminologist Walter Reckless (1933) makes the point that the dams constructed by the anti-vice movement were too weak to hold the avalanche of crime. Motion pictures, pulp fiction, and tabloid journalism fed on the stories of murder, sexual indiscretion, and white slavery. In cinema of the early 1900s D.W. Griffith produced a series of melodramas in which sex and violence were central elements. *The Musketeers of Pig Alley* (1912) was quite graphic for the time in its treatment of prostitutes, drug trafficking, and gang violence. This was followed by such ventures as *Traffic in Souls* (a story of white slavery) and *Devil's Needle* (a tale of addiction and crime). But it wasn't until the 1920s and Josef von Sternberg's *Underworld*, about the Chicago crime scene, that filmmakers began using some of the elements that would become the hallmark of American noir. Von Sternberg's work emerged from Weimar and German expressionist influences. He would go on to make such noir classics as *Docks of New York, Shanghai Express, Devil Is a Woman* and others.

Sex Everywhere

Changes in sexual attitudes and mores became central to the culture of early twentieth century America. A perceived openness in sexuality made its way into novels, magazine stories, psychology, and sociology proclaiming an end of the Victorian code of repression. Feminist scholar Christina Simmons (1992) notes:

> Intellectuals, bohemians, and radicals attacked Victorian middle-class mores in the first two decades of the century at the same time sexual behavior seemed to have been changing. Long-standing demands for female-controlled contraception—through voluntary motherhood and the right to say no—shifted toward a new demand for artificial means of birth control to facilitate female sexual pleasure as well as fertility control. Public discussion of these ideas signaled to both critics and proponents that more sexual activity was taking place inside and outside of marriage, an increase precipitated by changes in women's sexual attitudes and behaviors [p. 19].

The number of women living alone in cities like Chicago rose tremendously in the 1910s and 1920s. Women left home for a variety of reasons. Some were unmarried women suspected of sexual indiscretions (including homosexuality); others had been sexually abused (Meyerowitz 1988, p. 16). Like Theodore Dreiser's Carrie Meeber, many women ventured into Chicago simply to find work, to meet the challenges of urban life and to absorb its excitement and adventure. Like a great magnet, the city drew people to it for many reasons. But the woman alone in the city was seen as vulnerable—a possible victim and, if not a target, frequently mistaken for a prostitute.

Joanne J. Meyerowitz (1988) notes that these solitary urbanites were referred to as "women adrift." These were women not under the immediate control of their fathers, brothers, boyfriends, or lovers. Many lived in boardinghouses that developed to serve their needs. Women adrift became a phenomenon discussed in the tabloids, novels and magazines. Images of these women worked their way into the sociological narratives. Often such women were associated with liberated sexuality.

Sociology Noir

Hard-boiled fiction as well as scholarly sociology contributed in some meaningful ways to this reassessment of sexuality and the independence of women. Both explored changing sexual mores. Sociologists as well as writers of fiction engaged in what Greg Forter called "the privacy of a story too personal to be narrated straight "(Forter 2000, p. 3). For a rather staid segment of academia the study of prostitutes, unadjusted girls, and taxi dancers was a safe means of examining female sexuality as it emerged after World War I in its more powerful form. When framed as deviant behavior, aggressive female sexuality could be categorized and controlled. Hard-boiled fiction dealt more directly with male uneasiness in the face of such liberation. Sexually powerful women were often seen as femme fatales; the less sexually powerful were victims. Women were frequently objects of sadistic violence, or they were sadists themselves. Sometimes women became street-wise detectives, blurring the rigid boundaries of gender and revealing a streak of sadomasochism.

By the 1920s young women were no longer viewed primarily as bastions of innocence and virginity. New modes of dress accentuated the body. Shorter dresses, cosmetics, cigarettes, "once the styles of prostitutes," became more typical of the modern working-class woman (Meyerowitz 1993, p. 44). Liberal patterns of sexual activity were emerging. Women adrift were taking their place alongside solitary men in the city. "Loose women," flappers, and gold diggers (a more modern equivalent of vamps) entered into the iconography of novels and cinema.

In response to increased urbanization and the entrance of large numbers of young women into secondary schools and the work force, courtship patterns underwent significant changes. Kevin White (1993, p. 14) notes that the term "date" originated in the working-class enclaves of Chicago in the 1890s before being introduced into popular literature. Courtship, once centered in the home under strict female supervision, was transformed into a dating system in which there was much more freedom in terms of companion selection on the part of females. Marriage was not the aim in these short-term relationships. Such freedom led to a greater consumption of public entertainment shared by dating couples. Also, a new type of "charity girl" emerged. These were single women living alone who frequently exchanged sexual favors for being treated to gifts and nights out.

In the furnished room district of Chicago between the 1910s and 1930s, gender and sexuality were played out in radically new ways. Sociologists recognized these changes and went to work observing and recording them. Among these observers were Chicago school researchers Robert E. Park, W.I. Thomas and a number of their students. While some sociologists saw the rooming house district as a source of family decay and human alienation, many more saw it as an arena of the liberation and emancipation for women. Park and Thomas were careful not to alienate themselves from municipal vice commissions and conservative conformist organizations that provided some funding for their research. Nevertheless, they tended to view these changes as progressive. Both saw themselves as advocates of women's rights. Unlike their social gospel predecessors, they viewed change as "natural" and not something that signified the demise of society. They were both married to emancipated women. Park's wife, Clara Cahill, was an intellectual, artist, writer, and feminist, and Thomas's wife was in the forefront of the suffrage and peace movements.

By the early 1920s sex had made its way into the realm of entertainment directed to a wider audience than ever before. It had also become the subject of sociological investigation, taking its place alongside the subjects of poverty and race as topics to be explored by academics. Sexuality, as Foucault noted, was pushed into the open where it was better observed.

Slums and Slumming

Chad Heap's study of so-called slumming and thrillage in Chicago reveals that a commercial market had been established in the early 1900s for middle class tourist expeditions into poor neighborhoods for purposes of cultural enlightenment and personal entertainment. Heap (2000) uses the term *slumming* to denote middle class ventures into the bohemian underworld usually located in areas of great poverty in the city. While early excursions into immigrant strongholds and communities of otherness ranked high on the order of slumming priority as time passed, visits to illicit clubs located in the poor neighborhoods became a prominent urban pastime. Much was made of the worldliness gained from ventures into the urban ghetto and rubbing elbows with the hobo and the hoodlum.

The beginnings of organized bohemian groups in Chicago can be traced to the mid–1860s, but by the beginning of the twentieth century there were already established the Bohemian Club and the Cypher Club (Wilson 1991, p. 75). But by the early 1920s much of authentic bohemianism was gone. Still writers and artists gathered into neighborhoods near the old Chicago water tower, which went by the name Towertown.

A capital of alternative lifestyles and politics, this area of Chicago offered a new way of looking at the world. Here one could go to hear the speeches of incensed anarchists or the lectures of some of the most renowned public lecturers on matters ranging from sex to socialism. Towertown attracted lesbians and gay men whose lifestyles were accepted there. Similar in many respects to New York's Greenwich Village, it offered a cultural oasis to those seeking alternative answers. A variety of clubs sprang up, offering entertainment and cultural enlightenment.

The flow of visitors into Towertown and similar bohemian enclaves was beginning to break down the borders dividing legitimacy and illegitimacy. There was a growing interest in the changing mores of society, particularly sexual mores.

As Heap notes, "[S]lummers explored the marginality of these spaces, partaking not only of the rough and tumble atmosphere but also of their exotic possibilities" (p. 16). By the 1920s University of Chicago students were frequenting bohemian quarters of Towertown in great numbers. Many attended the various underground clubs that sprang up wherein one could meet prostitutes, hobos and free-loving bohemians, and discuss current topics such as homosexuality and revolution with burgeoning intellectuals, artists, and writers. Heap finds that homosexuality was explored by many graduate students of sociology:

> University students comprised a significant portion of the "slumming" crowd that nightly filled cabarets with queer reputations to overflowing—a fact confirmed by student reports on such resorts as "Dimond Lil's." Well aware that his students were participating in this nightlife phenomenon, Burgess urged them to transform their leisure activities into detailed sociological field reports by documenting the nightspots and drag balls they attended as well as the jokes and musical performances they witnessed in such spaces [Heap 2000a, pp. 21–22].

Free love, homosexuality, female impersonators, and live sex shows attracted the curious in increasing numbers. Smoke-filled clubs such as the Dil Pickle gained international renown and were crowded with radical poets and journalists who challenged the status quo and carried on political discourse long into the night. In keeping with its frontier reputation Chicago offered much to the curious sightseer. Prostitution, free love, and overt homosexuality also drew undercover agents from the Bureau of Investigation (the forerunner to the FBI), who were now charged with following and apprehending sex offenders, and keeping the sexually rambunctious proletariat at bay.

Criminology: Crime Fiction and Dark Cities

Chicago school sociology, under the leadership of Robert E. Park, ventured into the gloom of the poorest quarters of city. His students became urban detectives, pounding the pavements, invading dusty police and social service files, illuminating public vice and personal transgression.

In the early 1920s, Walter Reckless studied the vice areas of the city, Frederick Thrasher looked at gangs and gang life, Paul Cressey examined prostitution, and Clifford Shaw looked at juvenile delinquency. Park supervised many of these studies, as well as studies of immigrants and homeless men, identifying the Chicago school with studies of urban marginalization. Much of the data collected by these sociologists, including first-person accounts, came from interviews and newspapers—not the most reliable sources, but certainly ones favored by Park.

Chicago school analysis became more and more focused on seeing the links between social conditions and criminal behavior. It was assumed by many scholars, including Park, that crime was a social outcome and not an independent or aberrant condition. In order to understand criminal behavior, one had to comprehend the social conditions that led to its production. Getting into the streets in order to see it up close was eminently necessary.

Early hard-boiled fiction began to proliferate at approximately the same time the monographs started emerging from Chicago. Like sociology, it took many of its cues from the popular press. It was the crime saga and human interest pieces that roused the public's imagination. Hard-boiled writers like James M. Cain and Horace Stanley McCoy had both gotten their start as newspapermen, reporting crime stories for papers like the *New York World* and the *Dallas Dispatch*, not unlike Park himself. By the mid–1920s several pulp magazines devoted to the hard-boiled emerged. While the city of Chicago was not the center of this publication industry, it did produce its share of pulp magazines and pulp writers. Vincent Starrett, one of the city's more renowned pulp writers, worked for Chicago newspapers long before he published his first short stories. Eventually the city would come to house *Black Mask*, which had pioneered this work.

The ascendance of the University of Chicago as a major center of criminal research was conditioned by several variables. First and foremost, Chicago was a center of criminal activity, a node of organized crime and an arena in which the struggles of marginalized people were played out in its streets, factories, and tenements. It had been a place of violent labor disputes and race riots and the headquarters of several anti-vice groups. It contained a vast array of neighborhood gangs occupying a large variety of distinct ethnic neighborhoods. Geographically Chicago was a city of transience—a national crossroads, a congested labyrinth.

Park, Burgess, and Thomas sent their graduate students to explore and describe what they had seen. Many were deeply affected by their experiences. By interviewing their subjects, social researchers showed them to be complex human beings, not the one-dimensional figures frequently portrayed by the media. This complexity was a hallmark of Chicago school sociology, proletarian literature, and better hard-boiled fiction.

While sociology noir was not sensationalistic, it did border on it; it was brimming with human interest. Like hard-boiled authors, the sociologists who documented criminal activity focused on the ambiguity that was reflective of criminal life. Money, sex, and power were elements sociologists examined; these were the same driving forces perceived by writers of short stories in *Dime Detective*.

Hard-boiled sociologists were interested in the labyrinthine spread of crime into the nooks and crannies of city neighborhoods, into the tenements, bars, and flophouses; they were also curious about those who committed the crime and the circumstances that brought them to the act. Of course these weren't stories of the imagination, but some of the best narrated tales were assembled to capture the fascination of the reader.

The criminology of the 1920s and 1930s was of a cruder variety. Ernest Burgess, who was interested in identifying social variables on Chicago street maps, worked closely with a handful of graduate students to collect and organize data from police and social agency reports. He was able to get much of this work funded through various sources. However, those who had been trained by Thomas and Park were more likely to resort to ethnographic techniques. Thomas's interactionist perspective and Park's journalistic approach were to shape generations of scholars. Unlike Burgess's methods of social geography, or the survey approach taken by Charles Booth in London, this hard-boiled sociology delved into the murky psyches of the criminals themselves. It was this same psychological dimension that had invaded fiction and was now spreading throughout the Chicago studies. By the 1920s and 1930s, psychoanalysis had gained considerable currency in the United States.

Thomas's study of the unadjusted girl, Anderson's study of the hobo, Cressey's work with the taxi dancer, and Shaw's account of the jack-roller were important for their personal and often intimate human portraits. These scholars never abandoned the sociological elements that made their work relevant to policy makers, but they had come to realize that the understanding of social problems had to be based, in part, on a deeper familiarity with the personal core of those cast into the role of deviant.

A part of the socio-psychological dimension of criminology at the University of Chicago came from the powerful influence of George Herbert Mead, who taught the first generation of graduate sociology students there and whose work in psychology greatly influenced W.I. Thomas and the interactionist perspective. Mead's work focused on the social construction of the self and the social conscience, which he asserted originated in early acts of symbolic communication. The ability to take the role of another was essential to the socialization process. Through role taking and role playing, concepts of self and a generalized other emerged. Mead continually stressed the inner life of the individual as the source of personal understanding and overt social behavior.

Another important influence on the psychological dimensions of the Chicago ethnographies, particularly those dealing with social deviance, was the university's affiliation with the Institute for Juvenile Research (IJR). The IJR was originally founded as the Juvenile Psychopathic Institute, a state operated child study and guidance clinic under the direction of Dr. William Healy, who had studied with William James at Harvard. This organization was heavily endowed by Ethel Sturges Drummer, who was an advocate for the rights of delinquent girls and young women, but it gained most of its funding from the Illinois State Department of Public Welfare. Herman Adler, a former professor of psychiatry at Johns Hopkins University, was named as the IJR director in 1917. By the 1920s money was raised for new programs of clinical and behavioral research, and the institute attracted such active supporters as Jane Addams, Ernest Burgess, and George Herbert Mead. When Adler resigned his post as director in 1929, he was succeeded by Ernest Burgess. The IJR became an important center for crime research and employed a large number of Chicago sociology students (Bulmer 1984, p. 124).

It wasn't until the 1930s that there arose a stronger link between the fictionalized portrayal of the urban underbelly and the sociological accounts. Sociologists who worked for the IJR, such as Nels Anderson, Paul Cressey, Frederic Thrasher, and Clifford Shaw, wrote expressively about the lives of young people caught in a web of crime. The depression years saw many writers come face-to-face with the misery of city life. While not hard-boiled in the traditional sense, writers such as James T. Farrell, James Wright, and Nelson Algren described the down-and-out of Chicago. These writers did not focus on city detectives, but rather examined the urban psyche under stress and the struggle to maintain a sense of humanity in an increasingly corrupt world. They looked at urban society in turmoil and the breakdown of family life. All had studied sociology in one form or another. Farrell attended the University of Chicago as an undergraduate and took courses in sociology. He was very much influenced by the work of Mead and Thomas (Landers 2004, p. 53). Wright developed a friendship with Louis Wirth and his wife. In fact, Mary Wirth (Louis Wirth's wife) was Wright's social worker. She helped to secure his first paid job as a hospital orderly (Fabre 1973). Algren never attended the University of Chicago but was very much influenced by the Chicago school sociologists; he knew Louis Wirth from the John Reed Club and the Illinois Writers Project, and eventually taught a writing course at the University of Chicago (Drew 1989). These authors' renditions of urban deviance were gritty and real, yet reflected a sophisticated understanding of the roots of the problems.

Many came to know one another through their membership in the aforementioned John Reed Club of Chicago, which was a communist affiliated group that sponsored readings, workshops and lectures dealing with issues of poverty and race. Also, they all secured jobs in the 1930s in the Illinois Writers' Project, which was a part of the WPA. Louis Wirth, very active in the project and a regular lecturer at the Reed Club, helped to influence these writers by suggesting methods for the collection of information on city life (Drew 1989, p. 101). Unlike detective fiction writers, these Chicago writers took a hard look at the problems of poverty, prostitution, delinquency, and addiction.

Carla Cappetti (1993), in a detailed study of the influence of the Chicago school on these writers, reveals a wealth of evidence on just how these authors were affected by their sociology teachers. She cites courses taken, papers written for courses, and teacher-student friendships that had both direct and indirect influences on these writers:

> The trilogy of *Studs Lonigan* by James T. Farrell, *Never Come Morning* by Nelson Algren, *Black Boy-American Hunger* by Richard Wright ... cannot be understood within a restrictively literary context—proletarian, ethnic, naturalistic, or otherwise—but must as well be framed within a larger tradition of urban writing. Central to this tradition are the sociological writings, theoretical and empirical, on the city, produced by Chicago urban sociologists just before or at the same time as these novels and autobiographical narratives. Characters in books by Farrell, Algren, and Wright walk along the same streets that the sociologists charted, joined the gangs that they studied, encountered problems that they explained, and came to the sorry ends they foretold [p. 2].

Cappetti notes that while the Federal Writers Project became famous for its state guidebooks, it was less known for its collection of folklore, interviews with workers, and neighborhood studies. Through the sponsorship of the Project ethnographic sourcebooks and manuals were prepared by some of the leading social scientists of the day and sent to each of the local state offices. These guided writers in their work for the Project (p. 168).

Just as these writers were impressed by their studies of urban sociology, Chicago school professors were equally influenced by these authors. Louis Wirth's daughter, Elizabeth Marvick, noted that the only popular fiction she remembers her mother and father ever reading were mystery novels and Farrell's Studs Lonigan books (personal interview with the author, 1981). Wirth's younger daughter, Alice Gray, remarked, "My mother never read a novel that didn't have a murder in it" (personal interview with the author, 1981). Both daughters noted that their parents were into "lowbrow" American literature.

Not only did Wirth's wife Mary help secure jobs for Richard Wright,

Louis Wirth also provided Richard Wright with a reading list in urban sociology and introduced him to Robert Park (Cappetti 1993, p. 185; Fabre 1973, p. 93). It was through Wirth that Wright began a collaborative relationship with Horace Cayton, who was also a friend of the Wirth family as well as an assistant to Wirth at the University of Chicago (Rowley 2001, p. 81). Another of Wirth's key assistants, Edward Shils, was a very close friend of Saul Bellow. Bellow was also engaged by the Illinois Writers Project (Atlas 2000).

The WPA held an important place in the lives of unemployed Midwestern writers, especially writers of hard-boiled fiction and proletarian novels. Although no comprehensive study has been done to date on the relationship of noir literature to the Writers Project, there is ample evidence that the connections ran deep. There is also considerable evidence of sociology's role in this connection, especially in directing these writers to look at the city in certain ways (Rowley 2001; McCann 2000; Polito 1995; Cappetti 1993).

Chicago school sociologists recognized that the men and women of the streets were struggling with the same problems they were. The Great Depression had hit the cities hard, and people were attempting to survive at any cost. The sociologists did much to humanize their subjects at the time.

It is clear that part of the demise of the one-dimensional criminal archetype must be credited to the social scientists at Chicago. Urban sociologists were not only speaking to other sociologists, but also through their connections with writers and local journalists they were communicating to a much wider audience. Public officials, foundations, the press, students, even the general public were influenced by what their studies revealed. By the third decade of the twentieth century, theories of Lombroso, Goring, and other positivists stressing mental and physical abnormality lost considerable creditability. While such analyses would never die, they gave way to more cogent narratives of urban realism.

Dashiell Hammett's work, which had been earlier eclipsed by a lighter, more playful gum-shoe style of mystery fiction, now found a wider audience. His protagonists seemed more complex, not in control. Coming through the same channels, such as *Black Mask* and *Dime Detective*, Hammett looked like an author with something to say about the social corruption surrounding him and the human condition in general. Unlike some of the less sophisticated writers for the pulps, Hammett had been powerfully influenced by Conrad, Dos Passos and others. These strong literary influences were evident in his work and captured the attention of literary critics. In some ways his writings complement those just mentioned. Realism, fatalism, and, nihilism are as deeply embedded in his characterizations of urban life as they are in some biographical narratives of Chicago monographs. There was something deeply sociological driving his stories.

By the 1940s, both criminology and hard-boiled fiction had significantly matured. World War II increased America's paranoia and cynicism. Men returning home from war carried with them a new suspicion if not disdain for political power. John Galliher (1995) has noted that post–World War II criminology at Chicago attracted older students, many of them veterans who were there because of the GI Bill. These were mostly working-class men who kept their idealism well hidden. They were distinct from other sociology students who were from more affluent families. Most did not intend to be academics, but were interested in the study of the social problems surrounding them. This is part of what has been identified as a second Chicago school (Gusfield 1995).

A Tradition of Chicago School Study

Criminologists and hard-boiled authors peeled back a veneer of civility, exposing the ugliness of poverty and the blood-stained pavements of the mean streets. Of course, descriptive sociology of this era was more sanitized, but it did approach many of the same issues raised by the narrators of dark cities and crime fiction.

Two of the people most responsible for the turn toward a more reflective criminology were Clifford R. Shaw and Henry D. McKay. Shaw and McKay had their start as graduate students in the sociology department at the University of Chicago where they studied with Robert Park and Ernest Burgess. In the early and mid–1920s their work began as ecological surveys, mapping of crime rates in various neighborhoods. But by the 1930s they began examining the socio-psychological conditions involved in producing criminal behavior. As John Laub (1983, p. 13) noted in his history of American criminology, "Shaw and McKay, in sharp contrast to earlier approaches, assessed broader social processes such as immigration, industrialization, and urbanization, and their effects on the breakdown of traditional institutions such as family, church, peer groups, and the neighborhood at large. They eventually moved from locating the causes of criminal behavior in social change and other social processes to emphasizing the significance of social structure in the production of anti-social behavior" (Firestone 1976, p. 93). In 1926, Shaw had been appointed research director to the Institute for Juvenile Research with the assistance of Ernest Burgess, who helped create the post for him. McKay, whom he met at the university and who was also a student of Burgess, became his research assistant in 1927. Their work moved criminology into new directions. Shaw, particularly, was interested in looking at the relationship between community and delinquency. Unlike McKay, who focused more on statistical analysis, Shaw, who had been a probation and parole officer, went into the streets to speak with young people involved in crime. *The Jack-Roller*, which will be discussed in greater detail later on, was an exemplary product of his biographical research.

The IJR became an important extension of Chicago school research. Shaw was very much in tune with the political climate of his day. He worked diligently to apply some of the earliest theories developed by Burgess at Chicago to understanding the increase in juvenile delinquency. In empirically identifying certain communities as areas of antisocial behavior, he helped establish what became known as the Chicago Area Project (CAP), which worked to involve people from disadvantaged neighborhoods in efforts to curb juvenile crime.

It was the finding of Shaw and McKay that neighborhoods characterized by economic distress, not simply high rates of immigration, were those that seemed to have the highest crime rates. By working within these communities and tapping into its creative human resources, it was believed that some of the factors conditioning these high crime rates could be better addressed rather than through established channels of social work and policing. Community organization became a strategy and a tool for reform. The Chicago Area Project was established as a delinquency prevention and research operation, launched by Shaw and staffers at IJR. Established in 1934, the year that the Rockefeller Foundation grant to the IJR was terminated, the Chicago Area Project carried on from where IJR had left off (Bulmer 1984, p. 124).

The CAP continued to maintain strong ties to the University of Chicago, employing a number of its graduate students in various research endeavors. At one time, Saul Alinsky, the renowned community organizer, was hired by Shaw to help organize a poor community near the stockyards. Shaw and Alinsky came into conflict over organizing strategies. Still, the material of Alinsky, Shaw and McKay was the same stuff woven into streetwise novels by Algren and Wright, and into dark fictions of Hammett and Chandler. Referring to this mélange, Carla Cappetti (1993, p. 158) notes that journalism, literature, and sociology blended together to produce important urban tableaux. These works seem to inform one another.

Chicago produced a goodly share of hard-boiled writers: Stephen Keeler, Clyde Clason, Jonathan Latimer, Craig Rice, and Donald Hamilton all had been based in the city. Hamilton's father taught medicine at the University of Chicago, and Hamilton himself took his undergraduate degree there in the mid–1930s (Skinner 1998, p. 281). While this is no evidence of a direct influence of Chicago sociology on noir thrillers, it does show that there are some interesting connections.

Field Work as Social Narrative

The notion that Chicago social scientists themselves were detectives searching for clues has some degree of currency but has not been substantially developed (Schwanhaeusser 2002). The salient connection between noir fiction and noir sociology is a shared reassessment of the world wherein so-called deviants become human beings, not shallow statistical representations of social problems, or psychopaths, or stereotypical villains. Unlike the scientist-detective—detached and critical—the Chicago ethnographer often became connected to the subject in a personal way. Walter Reckless was known to play the fiddle with bands in the roadhouses he studied while socializing with pimps and prostitutes (Martin 1990, p. 180). Park, Shaw, Wirth, and others frequently befriended their subjects and integrated them into their lives—sometimes taking people into their homes for dinner. The deviant began losing its position as a pejorative object, and deviant behavior became the more accepted subject of study.

The Chicago monographs were more than a collection of empirical studies examining urban phenomena. They were important explorations of people living at the edges of society. The authors of these studies attempted to humanize their research subjects by allowing them the freedom to describe their own experiences and the personal struggles that directed them sometimes toward socially unacceptable behaviors.

Field method was nothing new. It had long been a central tool of social anthropologists. The use of field study in Chicago announced that what was being examined was something quite exotic. Researchers would go into places that "civilized" people dared not venture. It was certainly not as exotic as studying the Papua New Guinea Trobrianders. Often these urban inhabitants could be found around the corner and down the alleyway. However, the illumination of these dark recesses of the city was a pioneering venture for middle class social scientists just as it had been for tabloid journalists.

While Boas had a profound influence on the work of W.I. Thomas and the ethnographers who followed, it was the great Polish anthropologist Bronislaw Malinowski who emphasized field study among exotic populations, and who stressed detailed note taking and participant observation (Furth 1957; Kaberry 1957). Generally, ethnographic field work is viewed as a contextualized study of any group of people in a natural social setting. Many Chicago researchers similar to Malinowski put themselves into the worlds of others in order to capture a personal familiarity with those whom they studied. Unlike Malinowski, Chicago school researchers such as Thomas relied on personal documents, letters, and newspaper reports. Much of this might be referred to as "case study" (Hammerley 1989, pp. 67–72).

The narrative structure of these studies was what set them apart from European theoretical work, anthropological investigations, and social surveys of large numbers of people depicted in tables and graphs. As an art form the monographs emulated the best literature of the day; they were often driven by what Max Weber referred to as *verstehen*—a quest to understand human behavior in terms of feeling, motivation and spirit. These descriptive case studies of people who were trapped in urban ethnic enclaves of poverty and crime resonated with other stories of the streets. Emerging from a sociology attempting to define itself, the Chicago school monographs captured the imaginations of people from various segments of society.

What made Chicago school field studies so endearing was that they lacked pretense. They were concrete, pragmatic, and eschewed grand theoretical formulations and blame placing. The University of Chicago produced a whole host of scholars who aimed to explore, describe and understand the colorful and often dangerous world in which they lived. They frequently used statistics, charts, and graphs to present their data. Yet, beneath a hard exterior of positivist social science dwelt a softer center of subjective understanding—what Weber called *verstehen*. Indeed, this was the essence of hard-boiled sociology.

Conclusion

This city of Chicago became the backdrop for sociological stories that rivaled those found in the tabloids or in D.W. Griffith's early urban melodramas. Chicago was the city wherein the drama of personal turmoil and social unrest came alive. Park, Thomas, Burgess and their students at the University of Chicago embarked upon a program of research and the mass production of narratives of personal marginalization and studies on what they often described as social disorganization. Their work not only influenced and complemented the work of urban novelists and writers of noir fiction, but also frequently rivaled it.

These ethnographies became significant in that they captured a moment in the history of American urbanization. They looked at life in the slums, at juvenile delinquency and at gang behavior. In comparison to writers, artists, and poets of this era, Chicago school sociologists produced real life stories of people struggling against poverty and the lure of crime in the storm of social change. While many of these stories were bleak, they revealed a glimmer of optimism and some hope for the future.

It is in celebration of this work that the following renditions of urban life are presented.

Chapter 3

W.I. Thomas and the Unadjusted Girl

IN JOSEF VON STERNBERG'S FILM *The Blue Angel* (1930), a professor becomes infatuated with a nightclub performer and seductress, Lola Lola (played by Marlene Dietrich), who leads him on only to humiliate him, abandon him, and wreck his career. Written by Heinrich Mann, the brother of Thomas Mann, the story is set in Weimar Germany where sexuality takes interesting turns and reveals the loosening of the moorings of the Victorian era. The film, however, stands as a sort of cautionary tale—a warning about the power and danger of the sexually liberated woman and the erosion of western masculinity. Critics around the world read into this movie a commentary on moral corrosion and social disorganization.

Years prior to the film's release, American institutions were attempting to fight back the sexual changes that were shaking their patriarchal foundations. The tragedy of W.I. Thomas was that, although he understood the sexual revolution that was taking place and was indeed an important part of it, his teaching career came to a crashing end on the crumbling bulwark of American Puritanism.

This chapter explores Thomas's unique contribution to understanding gender, sexuality, and deviance from a distinctively situational perspective. His fascination with sex, and deep fondness for it—especially in its marginalized forms—was much more than many of his sober colleagues could bear. To have been discovered in a hotel room with a 24-year-old married women (he was 55 and married) caused the press to challenge that Baptist institution where he had made his livelihood.

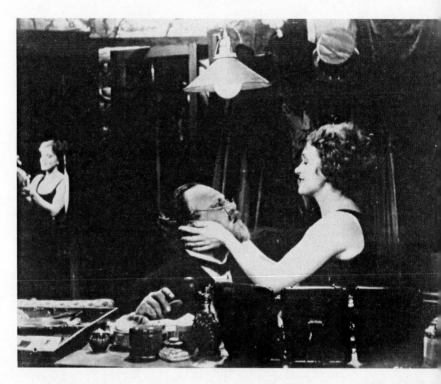

Marlene Dietrich, as cabaret siren Lola Lola, seduces Prof. Unrat played by Emil Jennings in *Blue Angel* (1930). The film dealt with the danger inherent in the emerging sexual power of women.

Thomas was no Professor Unrat. He was no worm-like curmudgeon infatuated with an untamed cabaret singer. If anything, Thomas was a decisive, sophisticated, and charismatic figure who could entrance both women and men from the most diverse social classes. It was he who helped to bring esteem to the university's innovative sociology program. His outstanding organizational skills, colorful personality, and creative intellect were used to advance his own career and bring renown to Chicago school sociology. Admired by his students and respected by his colleagues, one is frequently amazed at how his university career could be destroyed by such an affair of passion.

Thomas was one of the most influential sociologists of the last century. His "situational analysis" became one of the most important paradigms in American social thought and unintentionally helped to launch a subjectivist revolution in modern social science. He influenced generations of social theorists and moved Chicago sociology away from a moralistic social gospel and social reform focus and further away from mechanistic Darwinian and ecological models. His integration of ethnographic methods into his work was innovative and seminal. His interest in marginalized people prefigured his own banishment from the university and his life as an outsider.

Sketch of a Life

Little is really known about W.I. Thomas. While there are some short biographical sketches of his life and career (Janowitz 1966; Coser 1977), almost all of his papers, correspondence, and memoranda never found a home in a university archive. Whether they exist remains an open question. It was as though his life was expunged from the records at the University of Chicago—a place in which he matured as a scholar and with which his name remains forever associated.

William Isaac Thomas was born in Russell County, Virginia, on August 13, 1863. He recounts that this was a very rural and isolated area, nearly twenty miles from the nearest railroad spur. He was one of seven children. His father, Thaddeus Peter Thomas, was a farmer and sometime preacher in the Methodist church. Thaddeus rejected many of the narrow prejudicial attitudes of his own father and, against family wishes, attended Emory and Henry College. This rebellion not only brought on parental disapproval, but also resulted in a reduction in his land inheritance.

In an attempt to educate his own children, Thaddeus Thomas moved his family to Knoxville, Tennessee, the site of the state university. It was in Knoxville that William Thomas spent most of his childhood and early adolescence. His primary form of recreation was shooting and hunting and he often went into the woods alone. He seemed to enjoy the solitary nature of these regular excursions.

Although he began his undergraduate studies at the University of Tennessee in 1880, it was not until his junior year that he became a serious student. He majored in literature and the classics, taking courses with influential professors in the natural sciences and in classical Greek.

He was a popular student, won honors in oratory, and became president of the school's literary society and captain of its officers' training program. He remained at the university for his graduate studies, became an instructor of languages, and in 1886 was awarded the first doctorate ever granted by the University of Tennessee. Upon graduation, he remained at Tennessee where he was named an adjunct professor.

As with most young academics of this era, Thomas aspired to receive a German education. He wanted to tour Germany and to absorb its intellectual life. German universities were deemed superior to those in America at this time, so between 1888 and 1889, he took a year's leave of absence from teaching literature and traveled to Berlin and Goettingen. There he furthered his studies in language, taking courses in old English, old German, and old French. However, at the same time, he became fascinated with the ethnographic research of folk psychology, which was popular in Germany at the time. This resonated with his own interest in the relationship between linguistics and culture. Through the groundbreaking work of Moritz Lazarus and Heymann Steinthal, *Volkerpsychologie* became an influential way of looking at the ethnically diverse world. It would have a profound impact on the work of Georg Simmel, and Wilhelm Wundt, the founder of experimental psychology. It would significantly influence Thomas's work.

Underlying folk psychology was the notion that truth could never be discovered in *a priori* abstractions, but could only be discerned through psychological investigations that reached beyond individual consciousness into a social and cultural understanding of the world. Only by comprehending the diversity of cultures that constitute human existence and gaining insights into meaning attributed through language, customs, and myth could one achieve valuable understandings about people and their consciousness. Folk psychology promoted the notion that knowledge, tendencies, and experiences are stored in the mind in the form of dispositions; and that these dispositions are distinct from each other, although they are connected to each other and to cognitive processes in general. Folk theories of the mind often attempted to interpret and explain behavior through these dispositions. The evolution of culture in relation to environmental characteristics is seen as shaping these dispositions. Thus this study frequently degenerated into racism, and was often a platform for race theory—as was much of early anthropology.

Folk psychology was an attack against individual positivism and the scientific assumptions promoted in natural philosophy. It borrowed extensively from anthropology, and examined the mental products of so-called primitive peoples. Still, it had much to offer social science. Wundt's work in folk psychology stressed the importance of language and saw it as the key to understanding thought. In this sense, one might say that folk psychology, along with structural linguistics, was important for advancing what is frequently referred to as the linguistic turn in the social sciences. This, too, was to have a profound impact on Thomas's work.

When W.I. Thomas arrived back in the United States in 1889, he was offered a teaching position in the English department at Oberlin College. There he taught literature from a comparative perspective. He also began delving into social science, reading Herbert Spencer's *Principles of Sociology*. It was shortly thereafter that he decided upon a career in sociology.

Thomas had been reading news accounts about the opening of the University of Chicago and its offerings in sociology and anthropology. He believed that this could be his new calling; and so he took a leave from his position as a university professor to enter the graduate program there.

Thomas in Chicago

Thomas moved to Chicago in the summer of 1893 (Janowitz 1966, p. xii). There he worked under the supervision of Albion Small and Charles Henderson as part of the first wave of sociology graduate students. He did not limit himself to sociology courses, however, and he did considerable work in anthropology and the natural sciences. After a year of graduate training, he began teaching his first course in the program in the summer of 1894, giving up his professorship at Oberlin. By 1895 he was given the title of instructor and was assigned a full-time teaching load. He was awarded his doctorate in 1896. His dissertation was entitled "On a Difference in the Metabolism of the Sexes."

The University of Chicago was becoming one of the most prominent centers of higher learning in the nation. Its faculty included some of the most important scholars of the early twentieth century. Thomas was given an opportunity to study as well as teach along side of them.

Many who study Thomas's work cite his influences as philosopher John Dewey, psychologist George Herbert Mead, and psychiatrist Adolf Meyer, all of whom taught at Chicago. He was also deeply influenced by the anthropology of Franz Boaz.

Mead's work seemed to have had a significant impact on Thomas. Mead's psychology stressed the conscious mind. He believed that self-awareness was central to understanding human behavior. He emphasized the importance of language and symbolic communication in his work. It was symbolic interaction that freed humans from natural determinism. Thus, much of Thomas's interactionism, his focus on perception, as well as his understanding of the importance of personal interpretation in determining human behavior became an essential part of his definition of "the situation." Yet it is very difficult to evaluate the depth of influence of Mead on Thomas, since each man influenced the other.

It would be a serious error to say that Thomas took Mead's ideas and gave nothing in return. In his study of Mead, David L. Miller (1973, p. xxvii) notes that Mead would frequently refer to Thomas's work in his own lectures. In fact, while Thomas was a student of Mead's the two men developed a strong personal relationship and became close friends. They both held doctorates and were nearly the same age when Thomas studied with Mead. It would be more accurate to say that they influenced each other.

While the ideas of Mead, Dewey, Boas and, eventually, Jane Addams seemed to have had a formative impact on him, he frequently fails to cite many of these influences and claims to have influenced their work more than they influenced him. In speaking of Dewey, Thomas notes:

> When he came to the University I was already offering a course in Social Origins. I gave him materials used in his address as President of the Philosophical Society about that time and it would be more correct to say that he came under my influence than I came under his [Baker 1973, pp. 245].

Thomas worked his way into a position of prominence in the department. In 1900 he became an associate professor and then professor in 1910. During these years he grew close to Small and Henderson. He participated in the civic and social life of the city, and became a central figure of the Chicago school. Along with his wife, Harriet Park, he developed close connections with Jane Addams at Hull House. In 1908 he helped to create a new foundation with $50,000 from a local heiress,

3. W.I. Thomas and the Unadjusted Girl

Helen Culver, whom he had met through his affiliation with Hull House. This was the Helen Culver Fund for Race Psychology. Since the cost of Ford's new model T for this same year was $850, which was the equivalent of the average worker's salary for two years, $50,000 was no meager sum. Much of this money was used to support his own research on Polish immigrants, his trips to Europe, and what some considered a colorful lifestyle.

His strong interest in race, which was grounded in his reading of evolutionary theory, anthropology, and folk psychology, brought him to the attention of Booker T. Washington, who was organizing a conference in Tuskegee on that topic in 1910. Thomas noted:

> I received a letter from Booker Washington which resulted in an important influence. Mr. Washington wrote inviting me to participate in a conference where Negroes from 21 countries were to be present. He further went into an analysis of my printed work, disclosing the fact that he had read everything I had written and offering some criticisms and appreciations. As a result I attended this conference at Tuskegee and discovered that this letter was not written by Mr. Washington at all but by a white man, Robert E. Park. This was the beginning of a very long and profitable association [Quoted in Baker 1973, p. 249].

Thomas saw in Park a kindred spirit. The two men got along favorably, leading Thomas to invite Park to Chicago to give a series of lectures on race.

Park had been Washington's secretary, publicist, research assistant, and general administrator between 1905 and 1914 at the Tuskegee Institute. After his meeting with Thomas in April of 1912, he began his university teaching as a lecturer at Chicago in the fall quarter of 1913. He was forty-nine years of age. However, his full-time appointment did not commence until after Thomas was dismissed from the university in 1916.

Robert Park worked closely with Thomas and Albion Small. Small ran the department with help from Thomas, upon whom he now relied for many things. Unlike Henderson, who worked both as the university chaplain and the liaison with church and reform organizations, Thomas worked closely with Charles Merriam of the political science department and oversaw much of the funding of research projects in sociology (Karl 1974). His connections to public agencies in the city helped the department achieve many of its goals.

Thomas became active in civic affairs (and eventually personal ones).

He and his wife joined forces with Jane Addams, advocating for the rights of immigrants and women. Harriet Thomas became a founder of the International League for Peace and Freedom and was active in the International Suffrage Alliance, both of which had been targets of U.S. Department of Justice investigations (Bussey and Tims 1980). Thomas also found himself in opposition to the First World War and supported his wife's involvement in both of these organizations as well as Henry Ford's Peace campaign. W.I. Thomas's views became increasingly more progressive, and much has been made of his radical take on social deviance. He gradually rejected the biological determinism that was prevalent in social science and substituted a more constructivist vision of social relations.

Evolution of Scholarship

While many scholars pay particular attention to Thomas's contributions to interactionism, and, more specifically, to his notion of "definition of the situation," few have examined these ideas in context. That is, the essential elements of his interactionism are contained not in his older work, such as *Sex and Society* (1907)—a collection of essays written toward the beginning of his sociological career—but in *The Unadjusted Girl* (1923), a more modern narrative about prostitutes, unfaithful wives, and women craving physical intimacy, written considerably later.

If we look at Thomas's earlier contributions to sociology, we cannot fail to see a substantial amount of work dealing with human sexuality that is grounded in biological discourse. This was certainly part of the nineteenth century "discursive explosion" of which Foucault (1978) spoke in his history of sexuality. It was Thomas's original supposition that sex, like race, was embedded in nature, that men were physically "restless" and interested in sex, and women were physically "passive" and "stationary" and interested in children (Thomas 1963):

> In view of his superior power of making movements and applying force, the male must inevitably assume control of the life direction of the group no matter what the genesis of the group [p. 67].

One can read into his earlier work on both gender and race a biological determinism frequently associated with racist and sexist science of the day. He made little distinction between gender and sex. It was his early conviction that gender was driven by genes and endocrinology; that races and sexes were inferior and superior to one another because of their position in an evolutionary hierarchy. Based on this science, he originally accepted the notion of the natural dominance of white males and frequently noted that women were physically closer to children and to the "lower races" than to men (Thomas 1974, pp. 251–275). While some of this racism and sexism was tempered with progressive ideas on the relativity of physical aptitudes of the groups he compared, his early work was saturated with stereotypes and disturbing incongruities grounded in natural law and passed-off as social science.

In the earliest chapters of *Sex and Society*, he makes extensive use of Lombroso, but later he criticizes the notion of innate superiority of males and writes of the adventurous spirit of women, becoming quite critical of how males have attempted to dominate and subjugate females. In the later chapters, he moves away from natural law explanations and toward socio-psychological ones.

Some feminist scholars have focused primarily on Thomas's support for women's suffrage and equal rights and have ignored the biases inherent in his early work (Klein 1989; Deegan 1988; Rosenberg 1983). Though his ideas changed significantly over time, nonetheless they were part of the ongoing discourse grounded in a long tradition of maintaining strict boundaries between parents and children, men and women, straights and gays, whites and blacks. Such biases were not uncommon to educated men of his generation. However, as Thomas matured, his work became consistently more liberal in tone. He notes in a personal reflection: "I was about 40 years old before I assumed a critical attitude toward books and opinions" (Baker 1973, p. 248).

By the early 1900s he was championing the rights of women and African Americans. An examination of the evolution of his work, particularly in the area of sexuality and gender, reveals a continual and incremental distancing from reliance on Spenserian evolutionism and biologisms (Balfe 1981).

Thomas's turn to the personal biography of his subjects, initially in his work on the Polish peasant, was a departure from the type of work he was formally doing. It was closer to the ethnological research and cultural anthropology that fascinated him while he was studying in Europe. In Chicago, his work with social workers at Hull House and with William

Healy, who was the director of the Juvenile Psychopathic Institute (which later became the Institute for Juvenile Research), brought him into contact with people engaged in writing case histories and life stories of rebellious young people and struggling immigrants who dwelt at the margins of society (Lindner 1996, p. 138). It has been proposed that he made extensive use of the *Grosstadt-Dokumente*—fifty-one volumes, which were published in Berlin between 1904 and 1908 (Jabzinsek, Joerges, and Thies 2001). And the library records at the University of Chicago reveal that he was very familiar with these particular portraits of the marginalized urbanites, which, according to some, helped to give shape to *The Polish Peasant* and influenced the course of American sociology.

Thomas, like Park, was fascinated by outsiders. Being surrounded by establishment clergy, such as Small and Henderson at Chicago, he must have felt something of an outsider himself. Polish immigrants were accessible to Thomas. Their plight seemed to resonate with something inside of him. Still, in a letter written in 1935 to Dorothy Swaine (the woman who would become his second wife long after his dismissal from the university), Thomas notes that "The Poles are a very repulsive people on the whole...." He then writes in script above this evaluation: "difficult group to study," as though he is modifying this defamation (Letter from Thomas to Swaine, January, 1935, EBPA, Box 49, Folder 13). This disdain for his subject seems to reach into the depths of his innermost self.

Thomas saw Poles every day in the city as they packed into settlements in what was called the Polish Downtown—an area near Chicago's Division and Ashland avenues. It was there that the former peasants settled and began to build neighborhood institutions, in some ways recreating what they had experienced in the small villages from which they had come. Between 1890 and 1910, the Polish population of Chicago jumped from 40,000 to 210,000 (Kantowicz 1995, p. 174).

This research moved Thomas further away from the theoretical ruminations that occupied the early part of his sociological career. He was becoming much more of a pragmatist, more of a researcher—working closely with public agencies and the courts, collecting and interpreting data. His analyses were often psychological—more intuitive. His research methods were unconventional and used letters and diaries of the immigrants themselves, who told their own stories.

While *The Polish Peasant* established Thomas as a seminal researcher, few have paid attention to the role of sexuality, gender, and deviance in this work. Because of this deficiency, it is important to examine this work in terms of these elements so as to discern the true uniqueness of the Chicago school monographs.

Sex, Deviance, and the Polish Peasant

The Polish Peasant in Europe and America was a monumental undertaking. Thomas originally conceived of a study of transplanted immigrants upon a visit to Europe in 1896, after receiving his doctorate in sociology. It took several years before the project came to fruition. According to Thomas, the impetus for his method of research in part came from the discovery of a letter on a rainy day in an alley in back of his house. It was a discarded letter from a young Polish girl who was in a hospital training school to her father concerning family discord. "It occurred to me at the time," noted Thomas, "that one would learn a great deal if one had a great many letters of this kind" (Baker 1973, p. 250). To some extent, it was this curiosity (some might say voyeurism) that launched a project involving two continents and hundreds of letters, reports, and case studies. Of the nearly 2,250 pages of manuscript, approximately 60 percent of it is comprised of quotes and citations from these various documents (Smith 1988, p. 102).

The focus on poor immigrants, peasants, and those of the lower urban classes was becoming a hallmark of Chicago research. The lives of poor people were already dramatized in a great number of literary works of the day; in films, and in stories in the proletarian press. Thomas was familiar with much of this. Jane Addams, Edith Abbott, and Sophonisba Breckinridge had already called attention to the dire circumstances under which poor people lived by researching some of these problems in Chicago. City agencies did the same, but with specific policy issues in mind.

The Polish Peasant came to represent one of the seminal works of Chicago school sociology. It was a prototype for research that would follow. It seems to have been Thomas's intent, in launching this daunting project, to examine the transplanted peasant in a busy metropolis and to shift sociological research more to the realm of social psychology. While he originally planned to look at many diverse national European groups, he scaled back the project to examine only Poles. Peasants represented more than 60 percent of the Polish population at the time. It was they who would define the Polish nationality in the United States. But it would be much easier examining their lives than lives of the middle class. The poor always constituted a more accessible object of investigation. Issues of privacy and ethics of research did not apply there. Also, it was a subject of great interest in the popular culture.

Thomas was assisted in this venture by the extremely competent Florian Znaniecki, a Pole whom he had met on a research trip to Warsaw in 1913. Znaniecki was working there in the office of the Society for Protection of Immigrants and helped to secure documents for Thomas. Eventually Znaniecki joined Thomas in the United States, where he helped him with the project (Znaniecki 1948, p. 766).

In studying the lives of peasants thus transplanted, Thomas was focusing on the transition from communal life characterized by family and tradition to an individualistic one characterized by personal alienation and social pathology. He was also extremely interested in the whole notion of desire, or what he referred to as wishes. For Thomas there were four major wishes: security, new experiences, recognition, and affection or intimate association. These played themselves out in all social relationships, and in fact were seen as accounting for most human interaction.

Little in the way of class analysis can be found in this work, and there are credible reasons why his early work has been classified as an extension of the American syndicalist tradition—one wherein homeostasis is central to human progress that is achieved under a capitalist state (Schwendinger and Schwendinger 1974).

For Thomas and Znaniecki (1958) and others who looked at intimate human relations, sexuality in the metropolis, which once was relegated primarily to marriage, becomes detached from the traditions of familial life and the institutions that once supported it:

> Sexual desire, maternal instinct, in a much smaller measure paternal feeling, desire for response and desire for security are practically the only powers which draw and keep couples together. Our documents will show that none of these attitudes is sufficient to form a permanent basis for the family [p. 1704].

Thomas recognizes that sexuality is now forever uncoupled from marriage, both in the peasant family and for all who are a part of modern urban society. In example after example there are incidents of marital indiscretion, wandering, and divorce among transplanted Polish peasants. Couples in cities are free from the bans of the church, which loses its power, and free of each other due to the decline of the constraints of tradition. Monogamous marriage is given a short life expectancy for this group. There is excitement and adventure in sexual encounters outside of the marriage bed. And Thomas questions monogamy for American society as a whole. In fact, he sees monogamy as biologically unnatural and adhered to primarily for social and sentimental reasons (Thomas 1974, p. 193). He claims that while monogamy might claim our respect because of its current value to society "it reinforces relegating women to the home, which is irrational, antisocial and immoral" (Thomas 1908, p. 549).

The girls from these peasant families are particularly "loose" sexually. Lacking social education, they rebel against the seemingly tyrannical impositions of familial life void of purpose. They seek adventure, stimulation, and intimacy not available to them at home. Also, these young women tend to imitate their parents' lack of discretion in sexual matters and frequently fall prey to seduction of young boys and older men. Often they are swayed by money, entertainment, and material things. Some turn to prostitution. "The sexual immorality of most of the girls here described," notes Thomas (1958), "is thus in most cases a part of a generally unorganized life..." (p. 1817).

While Thomas makes it a point to assess female sexual activity, he looks at male children of these families as displaying antisocial and criminal behaviors. "The process of social disorganization is continuous," he notes, "and increases in intensity rather than changes in character when passing from the first to the half-second and second generations "(p. 1777). Marital conflict and indifference to children are causes of delinquency in boys, just as they are influences for promiscuity in girls. Once held together by strong communal bonds, peasant families that migrated to America lose their moral foundation. While girls still share some common interests with their mothers, Polish boys have almost nothing in common with their fathers. Given the rejection of old world constraints, these young men "follow their instincts" and frequently come into conflict with those agencies attempting to impose order in urban society. Theft, rape, and murder are all avenues open to these "wild" boys who lack the influence of a stable home environment and proper social education to keep their passions in check.

These boys and girls and mothers and fathers are alienated from that which once gave meaning to their lives. There is both a sadness and a savagery here as peasant traditions are undermined by the conditions of modern urban living.

Drawing upon a wealth of reports and documents, including court transcripts, diaries and letters, Thomas delves into the character of sexuality among the peasant classes. Girls and boys are lost in the dark shadows of illicit lives of crime and sex.

Thomas draws upon first person narratives of these people to dramatize these findings. The language is vernacular of the streets revealing class and ethnicity of the speaker.

There is a great degree of unrest epitomized in the lives of immigrants and their children as they struggle to attain their material dreams. While girls and women act out sexually, boys and men act out with violence. A craving ensues for new experiences, which appear to guide the behavior of these people living on the margins between the traditional folk world and the modern urban one. This is a space that is quite familiar to Thomas, who spent much of his young life roaming the hills of rural Virginia clad in a coonskin cap and carrying his rifle. Now he writes as a detached city observer.

Sex and the City

As sex began making its way into popular discourse in the United States, it was frequently connected to motifs of urban vice and lawlessness. Cities were often viewed as cauldrons of corruption and low-life depravity. The loosening of sexual constraints, increases of young women adrift, the rise in the use of birth control and prostitution were graphically covered in the penny press, dime novels, and later in the tabloid press. Cinema and popular fiction made much of the perceived changes in sexual mores. Often the sexual liberation of women was portrayed as vice and perversion and a sign of civilization in decline. The same held true for men who sought sexual pleasures with other men, or women with other women. In fact, the laws of the time made nearly every sex act outside of procreative intercourse a criminal offense.

Many sociologists viewed urbanization as destructive of marriage, patriarchy, heterosexuality, and traditional community. And although they did not overtly speak of the loosening of sexual constraints (for women and men), they frequently meant just that when they spoke of social disorganization. The concern surrounding urbanization was frequently the loss of men's control over women, and the ebbing of female domesticity.

Mary Jo Deegan (1988) has shown that the Chicago school itself became an academic bastion of male dominance and power. Women were either purposefully excluded from the full-time faculty in sociology or relegated to the school of public philanthropy. They were frequently discouraged from pursuing doctorates. Sociology was a field dominated by men who controlled the research agenda and determined the tools that were used to conduct studies. The work there as elsewhere was dominated by the traditional male gaze, which for the most part contributed to the domination of women by men and portrayed women as objects. Deegan makes special note that Thomas was exceptional in that he embraced women's issues long before any of his male colleagues. He was particularly aware of women being subject to enormous stress as they encountered new opportunities for personal growth (p. 121). He also came to recognize that sex was a dynamic and ever-changing force, and a very powerful one.

In a series of articles written for *American Magazine* between 1908 and 1910 (Thomas 1908; 1908a; 1908b; 1909; 1909a) he defends the rights of women against an increasingly reactionary cohort of men who seek to relegate females to the home and deny them not only the vote but also any say in the development of themselves and society. He recognizes the need for women to be liberated from patriarchal confines, but also recognizes the challenges this poses to men.

As the twentieth century progressed, crime fiction was able to synthesize many of the elements popularized in the sensationalist media. Sex, deviance, and the redefinition of gender roles made their way into popular literature. The tabloid press, which had also been dominated by men and almost exclusively male editors, frequently looked at these changes as undermining standards of morality.

In some ways, the rise in the popularity of hard-boiled fiction, wherein the solitary male detective came to signify a new masculinity battered by the forces of unscrupulous bad guys and the femme fatale, was a response to the changing social conditions played out in big cities such as Chicago.

Pulp fiction was very important in both signaling social change and helping to bring it about. It indeed reflects a sense of the modern wherein the very structure of society, once taken for granted, becomes tenuous. Males are losing their moorings and their traditional roles and women are entering the urban work force in record numbers and gaining some sense of autonomy.

If American Prohibition of 1919 and women's right to vote gained in 1920 can be seen as capitulation to the forces of female reform and the powerful women's temperance movement, then the rise of organized crime and organized racism might similarly be viewed as white male reaction to a perceived threat to their power and masculinity. Certainly, the activities of the Klu Klux Klan increased significantly with the advancement in the rights of women and the influx of immigrants. And Klan heroes even made their way into movies, magazines, and early detective fiction. The Klan, too, came to represent alienated men who were losing their power over women (Blee 1991). Much has been made of this phenomenon as Klan narratives ran a course in early pulp fiction, including *Black Mask* (McCann 2000, pp. 39–86).

Organized crime and organized racism were powerful forces that attempted to fight back the image of the "poor worm"—the man who no longer holds his women and slaves in check. The iconography of the lonely violent or potentially violent white male was essential to film and fiction of the Wild West. Now, with the loss of the range cowboy, the city became the stage on which the masquerade of masculinity was carried out. It was down these mean streets, in these dark alleyways, that a new masculinity was born.

Tabloid versions of sex and violence find their way into the early work of hard-boiled fiction. Calculation, revenge, and bloodshed are images that appeared to sell both newspapers and books. These are tied into the newly created image of the modern alienated male. As Jopi Nyman notes in *Masculinity, Individualism and Hard-Boiled Fiction* (1997):

> Hard-boiled writing signifies masculinity not only in its themes but also in its use of conventions.... The stories not only celebrate masculine virtues of courage and heroism, but describe how masculinity is posited as a cultural norm and given linguistic rendering. By ranking masculinity and life outside the home well above femininity and domesticity, hard-boiled fiction creates a fantasy world where male characters operate not only without women but in opposition to them and other representatives of non-masculinity [p. 35].

3. W.I. Thomas and the Unadjusted Girl

Hard-boiled fiction, insists Nyman, deals with men's abilities to survive alone in a hostile world (p. 40). But what Nyman doesn't say is that, at the same time, these men are vulnerable as they confront the corrupt and violent world in which they must eke out an existence for themselves. There is self-questioning, often lots of self-doubt. In fact, at least one critic of this genre blasts these writers, including Chandler, as being pathetic homosexuals—promoting homosexual and misogynistic agendas (Legman 1963, pp. 68–70).

Yet there can be no doubt that the hard-boiled protagonist is a challenge to the standard and classic hero people expected to read about prior to World War I. As Megan E. Abbott (2002) notes, "As figures who walk on the social margins, on the perimeter of the white bourgeois patriarchal hegemony, hardboiled protagonists are situated repeatedly among the racially and ethnically abject." She goes on to say that this is where the Western adventure story and the hard-boiled detective tale part company: "the narrative structure of a white man moving through the spaces of 'the Other' betrays hardboiled literature's relationship to the Western and to the frontier literature of the previous century" (p. 94).

Whether sociologists read detective fiction or not is not deeply relevant. What is significant is that the social currents influencing popular culture were identical or nearly identical to those that helped shape early twentieth century American sociology. As elements of cultural reproduction, sociology and hard-boiled fiction communicated a particular set of values that lay hidden from plain view. Often one cannot easily tell a protagonist from the antagonist. The space in which they dwell makes this difficult. There is paranoia here, and a sense of impending doom. Naturalism is essential to plots in hard-boiled fiction, which almost always uses the city as its backdrop. There is perversion, corruption and illicit goings on.

The city of Chicago had a historic reputation for its crime, violence, ethnic and racial conflict, and sexual exploitation. Prior to the Great Fire it was the quintessential frontier town. It eventually became a center for tabloid newspapers, muckraking journalism, and outrageous corruption—corporate, governmental, and individual. It became one of the most important literary centers in the world in the early to mid–1900s. Labor unrest, radical politics, organized groups of wealthy citizens working to reduce the chaos and disorder were all part of a vibrant social mosaic.

71

That the city emerged as a prime subject for sociological investigation is no accident, nor was the development of one of the finest research programs in sociology at the University of Chicago at the turn of the century.

What appeared to intrigue sociologists were some of the same elements of urban life that interested authors of hard-boiled fiction. Again, it was the margins, the borders, the dark corners of the darkest alleyways located in the gloomiest and perhaps most dangerous parts of the city. It was the people of the streets. Not the middle classes which consumed Baudelaire, but the downcast, the survivors, the quick talkers. It was also the illegal and illicit, the notorious smoke-filled clubs that rose up in the seediest parts of town. It was life on the outskirts, where few ventured to go.

Chicago bohemianism was as notorious as the countercultures in New York. Towertown stood as a geographic symbol of cultural and sexual liberation. Like Greenwich Village, it flourished in the early 1900s. It was there that artists, intellectuals, and radicals came to commit themselves to lifestyles that had been marginalized and relegated to the status of deviant long before the Miracle Mile came into existence. In his classic monograph, *The Gold Coast and the Slum*, Harvey Zorbaugh devotes a chapter to this place in the city that became a refuge for "bizarre and eccentric divergencies of behavior" (Zorbaugh 1929, p. 87). Zorbaugh included homosexuals in his definition of divergences.

Tea rooms, radical bookshops, small innovative theatres, and artist colonies proliferated there. Like New York's Greenwich Village, this was indeed a cauldron of cultural innovation, of people pushing boundaries both sexually and otherwise. It became a space associated with free love and homosexuality, with transient sex and women's liberation. According to Zorbaugh, with the gradual passing of Towertown in the late 1920s as the only space tolerant of diverse lifestyles, "The Bohemian way of life becomes increasingly characteristic of the city at large" (p. 104). It was into this maelstrom of cultural and sexual dynamism that W.I. Thomas was inevitably drawn. He ventured into places that had been off-limits to so-called respectable sociologists.

Sex, Lies, and Crime

Early in his career as a sociologist, W.I. Thomas (1898) noted that the very first expressions of culture were mere incidental accompaniments to human sexual activity. It was his assertion that the instinct for hetero-sexual copulation, for the purpose of reproduction, disappeared early on in humans with the advent of memory and imagination. He fully under-stood that human sexual activity was much more diverse than had for-mally been assumed, and that *Homo sapiens*, more than any other species, exhibited an amazing variety of sexual relations even within specific cul-tures.

While his attraction to sexuality as an area of study first took on both biological and physical anthropological dimensions, he was even-tually drawn to the notion of human desire and how this found physi-cal expression in the social world, particularly in the urban social world. While he is still primarily remembered for his interactionism, perhaps his most important student, Ernest Burgess, remarked that he was a renowned pioneer in the study of sex. "The approach of Havelock Ellis was largely historical and encyclopeadic. Freud dealt with sex in its uncon-scious manifestations," noted Burgess. "Thomas, by contrast, was inter-ested in sex behavior as culturally conditioned and culturally defined." He went on to say: "His bent toward empirical study led him to take risks as a sociological investigator" (Thomas: A Biographical Note by Burgess in EBPA, Box 49, Folder 13, 7). But what were the risks?

Thomas became fascinated with sex. As noted earlier, his notion of four "wishes" that drive all social behavior in some ways speaks "desire." This is not far removed from Hegel's notion of desire or Freud's ideas on object directed cravings, or even Lacan's idea that our most intimate desire is driven by the superego. He dedicated much of his time explor-ing the private lives of people—something sociologists rarely did. Perhaps, as a sociologist, this was the risk.

More than most sociologists of his time, Thomas was influenced by psychology. Unlike classical scholars such as Emile Durkheim and Max Weber, who purposely wanted to distance themselves from psychology and who formulated what sociologists refer to as macro-order theories, or "grand" theories, dealing with the nature and dynamics of social struc-tures and systems, Thomas was deeply influenced and moved by the indi-vidual and his or her struggles in life. This interest brought him close to Mead and to Jane Addams, with whom he socialized and worked. He met Freud in 1911 when traveling in Europe and became familiar with all of his work and many of the writings of Jung. He helped to dissemi-nate this material to his friends and colleagues, including John Dewey and Robert Park, when he returned to the United States (Letter from Thomas to Park, May 16, 1912:REPPA, Box 14, Folder 7).

In 1910, the year he made initial contact with Robert E. Park and Booker T. Washington, he was recruited by Chicago's famed Vice Commission to study prostitution in the city He had already published *Sex and Society* and several articles on human sexuality. He was captivated by this subject and interviewed many prostitutes himself. Prostitution became more visible as Chicago became more gentrified. But beyond this, 1910 was the year that the White Slave Statute, or the Mann Act, was passed into law by the U.S. Congress.

The commission, which was organized under the direction of then Mayor Fred A. Busse, began by investigating female prostitution. It was one of the most comprehensive studies of this phenomenon ever conducted by a municipality. It is filled with statistics examining the extent of prostitution in the city, its causes, and the police corruption related to it (The Vice Commission of Chicago, 1970). The work of the commission eventually expanded to include what they referred to as male "sex perverts" and later encompassed an investigation into a "cult" of feminine men and female impersonators who performed at music halls and saloons (Heap 2000, p. 16). How much Thomas had to do with this report is uncertain. But there was much in it that shows his hand. The growth of prostitution related to repressive home conditions, and the poor pay of women who worked in the city's department stores spoke to the urgency of social reform. Thomas was part of a group that included Graham Taylor of the Chicago School of Philanthropy, Charles Henderson, Thomas's colleague in sociology, and a number of other academics and social work professionals. The commission was comprised of thirty men and no women. Many of these men came from the ministry and the business community. What is certain is that many of Thomas's progressive suggestions did not sit well with his colleagues and seemingly never made their way into the report. While the report proposed a number of recommendations that addressed the social conditions, it ultimately urged the Mayor to address these problems primarily through criminalization and called for an expansion of the powers of the U.S. District Attorney's office.

Thomas eventually blasted the intractable moral tone of the commission's recommendations. He wrote that their work merely justified and reenforced a conservative moral code and that the commission members could not see, or did not want to see, the changing world around them. "Traditions and customs, definitions of the situation, morality and religion are undergoing an evolution, and a society, going on the assumption that a certain norm is valid and that whatever does not comply with it is abnormal finds itself helpless when it realizes that this norm has lost social significance and some other norm has appeared in its place" (Thomas 1969, p. 230). He strongly opposes criminalization and incarceration as tools to combat "delinquency."

Thomas's involvement with this commission in 1910, however, gives evidence of his more practical approach to issues of sexuality prior to publication of one of his most important works, *The Unadjusted Girl*, in 1923. But before he would start on this work, he would teach courses in both social deviance and the history of prostitution (drawing upon his experience with the commission and his own personal research), publish a series of articles for progressive magazines and newspapers defending the sexual revolution that was taking place and, finally, lose his career and reputation in a sex scandal that would shake the university to its very core. The dismissal of Thomas from the University of Chicago is an important element of the story of the sexual revolution of the early 1900s.

That one of the most prominent sociologists in the United States could lose his position at a university on the *suspicion* that he had an extramarital affair appears in some ways absurd by today's standards. Yet, not only was he to lose his career, he also had to suffer the humiliation of his private life being bannered in the headlines of the tabloid press.

Thomas had indeed been responsible for organizing and developing what we know today as the Chicago school of sociology. This is not to denigrate Robert Park's enormous contributions, but if it were not for Thomas, Park would never have come to the University of Chicago.

There is much speculation on why Thomas was targeted by the federal agents and the Chicago press—speculation as to why his arrest in a Chicago hotel room with the twenty-four year old wife of an American soldier serving abroad in World War I was so well publicized. While some speculation circulates concerning Harriet Thomas being the actual object of the investigation because of her antiwar activities, the Mann Act was cited by the FBI to justify its involvement in the W.I. Thomas case (Janowitz 1966, p. xiv; Coser 1977, p. 535). Why did the city in which he lived for most of his life pursue this case, charging him and the woman with "disorderly conduct" when no disorderly conduct ever took place? Why did Thomas's story become front-page news in Chicago for nearly two weeks? Why were his wife, the woman with whom he was caught, and his children, targeted and hounded by the media? Why was he dismissed from the university on the basis of press allegations without ever receiving a proper hearing?

The Mann Act, passed by Congress in 1910, was spurred on by popular fear of so-called white slavery. This was, in part, the reason for Chicago establishing a vice commission. Drummed up by the popular press, large numbers of women in cities were rumored as being forced into lives of prostitution by bands of organized criminals who sometimes took these women across state lines and national borders. While there was some degree of evidence that such acts had taken place, it was wildly exaggerated in the tabloids. In fact, immigrants were portrayed as the cause of the rise in prostitution, especially in the pimping of young girls (Langum 1994, p. 18). The Mann Act became an instrument for furthering the expansion of the FBI, since there were few federal regulations warranting federal policing. Founded in 1908, the FBI developed rapidly after 1910 because it was cast into the role of a morals enforcement agency. The Mann Act became a way of the federal government insinuating itself into the changing moral landscape. As an agency, it was rapidly gaining a reputation as an instrument of American xenophobia.

Thomas had a reputation for living a somewhat flamboyant lifestyle for a college professor. As sociologist Lewis Coser noted, "he enjoyed the company of attractive women, mixed in bohemian quarters, and dined in posh restaurants as well as local dives. He was, as they say, a controversial figure" (Coser, p. 534). His wife, Harriet Park Thomas, was involved in civic activities. She was a steadfast supporter of suffrage and a woman's right to birth control. She joined the antiwar movement and participated in peace demonstrations. Like many so-called university wives, while her husband wrote and lectured about social change she was involved in attempting to make it.

It was in the early morning hours of April 11, 1918, that Thomas and a 24-year-old woman, Mrs. Pearl Granger, booked into the Brevoort Hotel in Chicago under assumed names as man and wife. The press reported several inconsistent versions of what transpired after this. According to some reports, Thomas and Granger were suspected by the hotel manager of not being married because of their disparity in age and, therefore, as required by law, reported this suspicion to federal agents (Chicago *Tribune*, April 12, 1918: 1). In another newspaper account, the couple left their suitcase with the hotel manager, who opened it and, finding its contents suspicious, reported this to the agents of the Department of Justice (Chicago American, April 12, 1918: 3). In any event, federal agents came soon after the couple checked into the hotel and arrested them. They were brought to a magistrate judge, who released the pair; the two then returned to the Thomas home, where Harriet Park Thomas welcomed them both and defended them against media attacks.

Reporters gobbled up this story. Front-page headlines appeared for the next several days that accused Thomas in his written work of attacking the sanctity of family and sexual monogamy and promoting absurd moral practices. Aside from taking his academic work out of context and presenting twisted versions of what he put forth as a scholar, they characterized him as a cult-like figure and his wife as an agitating pacifist and socialist. The press reported that he urged promiscuity for women, chided marriage as "verging on immorality," and was in many ways misogynistic. Aside from this, he was fifty-five and she was twenty-four.

Thomas attempted to defend himself by first denying the story when reporters confronted him at his home. However, he soon was issued a warrant by detectives who came knocking on his door and accompanied him to the police station. Warrants had been taken out on Thomas and Granger by agents of the U.S. Department of Justice and served by local police who advised them "not to blow town." The following is an excerpt from the *Chicago Sunday Tribune* dated April 14, 1918:

> Prof. William Isaac Thomas, lecturer on sociology and morals, entered upon a petulant mood yesterday afternoon when the front door in South Clark Street Station ground shut behind him. Uneasily, he paced back and forth, pulling at a cigarette. Then he spied a dark corridor and retreated from prying eyes.

The story goes on to recount that he had been able to protect Mrs. Granger from a mandatory appearance by keeping her at his home in the care of his wife. Thomas was able to provide the police with a letter from a physician describing Granger's poor health, so that they did not immediately issue her a warrant. However, he had to go through the day's ordeal pretty much alone.

> "Thomas for bond!" sang a desk sergeant.... Prof. Thomas appeared from his corridor of refuge. The key in the door turned and he walked out. An

officer took him to the office of the station. [Thomas was taken inside and quickly signed the bond.] A crowd of reporters flocked around. Prof. Thomas, apparently in an angry mood, shook his head defiantly at them and said: 'Nothing for you! Nothing! Leave me alone!' A big man broad of shoulder he shoved them aside and made for the open air. Outside he briskly struck out on South Clark Street, stumping along like a man in a passion.

Newspaper photographers had besieged the Thomas home that morning and later in the day. They followed Thomas from his residence to the police station and back again. At one point, his twenty-two-year-old son, attempting to protect his father, got into a scuffle with reporters as he emerged from their home. Tabloid journalists certainly presented a dramatic version of a story of a man caught in the public spotlight in an act of marital indiscretion with a younger woman. It appealed to the working-class readership that was already skeptical of the university intellectuals anyway. Much was made of the fact that Granger's husband was in the army, that she had a three-year-old son, and that her sister was a struggling actress, Della Rains, who visited with the pair regularly. Photographs of Rains, Thomas, and his wife were splashed across pages of the evening papers. Curiously, not one photograph appeared of Granger except when she made an appearance at their court hearing on the only charges

THE CHICAGO SUNDAY TRIBUNE: APRIL 11.

THE PROFESSOR'S LOVE STORY

Miss Rains Is a Vigorous Champion of Her Sister, Mrs. Pearl Granger, Who Was Arrested with Professor at Loop Hotel.

Della Rains

Prof. Thomas

The press harasses W.I. Thomas as he is discovered in a downtown hotel with a woman who is not his wife. The incident resulted in the destruction of his academic career.

brought against them—disorderly conduct. Her face was then completely covered in a dark veil. She seemed always to wear black. Reporters were filled with information about Thomas, much of which was wrong. But they reported it anyway.

At the university, President Judson had been out of town, so Dean of Faculty James R. Angell, Albion Small, and Martin Ryerson, president of the board of trustees, took the heat. No one defended Thomas. Thomas was contacted by the university administration and finally met with Small on Sunday, April 14, three days after the incident. The following statement by Dean Angell was placed into the minutes of a special board of trustees meeting, which was held on April 16, 1918:

> Mr. Thomas admits the false registration at the Brevoort Hotel, admits that he was in a bedroom with Mrs. Granger when arrested, but denies any overt immoral conduct at that time. Regarding their previous relations his statements are non-committal. Without admitting any overt acts, in general Mr. Thomas defends the right of the individual to live his private life in such a manner as he sees fit and without interference by any institution with which he is connected. In light of this position it seems doubtful whether he will present his resignation as he was told by Mr. Small he ought immediately to do. Acting under the telegraphic instructions from President Judson, and after conference with Mr. Reyerson, I sent by mail to Mr. Thomas on Sunday, April 14, a message reading: "President Judson telegraphs me to notify you that you are suspended from your University functions." [This was signed by Dean Angell.]

Also read into the minutes at this meeting was a letter from Harry Pratt Judson dated April 15, 1918, reemphasizing the points made by Angell and calling upon the Board to vote for the immediate dismissal of Thomas. Judson was still in New York on business and seemingly made no attempt to rush back to Chicago. While the resolution was unanimously adopted, a number of key trustees failed to attend the meeting (Board of Trustees Minutes, University of Chicago, c 1 Vol. 10, 1917-1918).

Newspapers, particularly the Chicago *Tribune*, continued to harass Thomas and his family in their home, which now included a curious coterie of Mrs. Granger and sometimes her sister. Granger remained protected by Harriet Thomas, who called the actions of her husband and the young woman "silly" and "foolish." But the young Granger admitted to the press her love for the middle-aged sociologist, frequently referring to him as her "daddy." "He is the possessor of all the wisdom of the ages," she said. "He knows the mind: he penetrates into one's secret chambers, into one's heart" (Chicago *Tribune*, April 13, 1918, p. 8). The press made much of this, suggesting that she was attracted to the brilliance of Thomas as a moth is attracted to the flame, and that this attraction "was to lead to her doom" (Chicago *American*, April 13, 1918, p. 1). Also, much was made of the fact that Granger's husband was an officer in the army, stationed in France—and it was wartime. She had a three-year-old child who was staying with her parents while she went in search of herself with this "weird" man of science. Carla Cappetti (1993) notes: "The heavy-handed symbolism of this scenario was unmistakable: fantasies of incest taboo, unspeakable sexual sins, betrayal of country, and sexual triangles could be made out behind the daily news accounts" (p. 88).

By the time their day in court had arrived (April 19), the Federal government had dropped its charges against Thomas and Granger. The only charge that had been filed by the local district attorney remained disorderly conduct. The maximum penalty could have been a $200 fine. But this law had often been used by the City to prosecute prostitutes. Thomas and Granger were defended by Clarence Darrow, who was now a nationally prominent figure. The court and its environs were filled with hundreds of women activists from both the peace and suffrage movements—supporters of Harriet and William Thomas. Spectators stood on tables and chairs to get a glimpse of the proceedings. The space was overflowing with photographers and reporters. Camera flashes exploded as Thomas, his wife, and Pearl Granger (heavily veiled in black) entered the courtroom. The proceedings were over in a flash. Judge Frank H. Graham presided. Presented with the evidence by both attorneys, he ruled that there was no evidence of disorderly conduct. The judge harshly reprimanded the prosecutor and called into question the application of that law in this case. The charges were dismissed. The courtroom burst into cheers and applause, but a career had been wrecked in record time and all reputations involved were severely damaged.

The federal attorneys, who were present in the courtroom, told reporters that they were still investigating Thomas, but they had no immediate plans to prosecute. The acting police chief, Alcock, called for new ordinances covering immoral relations, and cited the disorderly conduct charge as woefully inadequate. When the judge was asked if the couple could be tried for the crime of adultery, he said no, that adultery must be open and notorious. The disorderly conduct law, used to prosecute those who violated the city's moral code, suffered a blow. It was quite obvious that a minor battle to advance the cause of less retributive and invasive governmental practices toward its citizens was won in that court-room that day.

W.I. Thomas and *The Unadjusted Girl*

Thomas's reputation was in ruins. Still, he sought ways of continuing with his life—and with his work. He issued a lengthy statement to the press outlining some of his ideas on sexuality and personal freedom (Chicago *Daily Tribune*, April 22, 1918:15–16). But it was too late. His wife, Harriet, stood by him throughout the entire ordeal and even had the young, emotionally distraught woman remain under her care. She was excoriated by the press for this and her judgment called into question. But she did it in the name of all women and sisterhood.

When the press first asked Granger whether she had considered the impact of her affair with Thomas on Harriet Park Thomas, she responded: "I don't think you understand. Mrs. Thomas and the professor had separate interests. Theirs was simply a matrimonial alliance. Their romance contained no passion" (Chicago *Daily Journal*, April 12, 1919:1). While this sounded like a line any unfaithful husband might give his newly found object of affection, much historical speculation has circulated around the extent of sexual intimacies of the women at Hull House and among many of those involved in the early suffrage movement (Faderman, 2000). There can be no denying that this statement could have fueled further speculation at the time and might have called into question Harriet Thomas's sexual orientation.

Thomas was near the completion of *The Polish Peasant*, and still working with the University of Chicago Press, which published the first two volumes of the work. However, more was set to be released when the scandal hit the press. Despite some opposition at the editorial board of the press itself, the university ordered that all relations and negotiations with Thomas for this project be terminated (BUP, Box 21, Folder1). Thus some of the most important works produced by Thomas were never published by the University of Chicago. This included the completed *The Polish Peasant*, which was the prototype for future Chicago school studies. *The Unadjusted Girl*, published in 1923, should have properly been the first in a series of urban ethnographic monographs undertaken by that press.

But given the university's striving to disassociate itself from Thomas, Nels Anderson's *The Hobo* (1923) became the first book in this series.

Thomas's teaching career had come to an abrupt end. He had been teaching a course in the history of prostitution and collecting information for a book on this subject and on delinquency in girls. Suddenly, he was out of work. However, he continued on with his research. His friends did not abandon him, nor did he abandon them. Despite the vicious press attacks against both him and Harriet Park Thomas, they remained connected to politically progressive movements.

The Unadjusted Girl was the product of years of research and intense reflection. In it Thomas manages to weave together a variety of first person narratives that he was able to secure from women and girls from a number of public and private sources, including a set of letters written to the Jewish *Daily Forward* in New York. His book is groundbreaking on a number of levels. It is a work that speaks against the traditions of patriarchy that tied women and young girls to a life of domesticity. It addresses issues of youthful rebellion and shattered grown-up dreams.

Thomas now makes clear his previously sketchy rendering of the four wishes or desires that he proposes rules the lives of everyone. He uses the word "desire": the desire for new experiences, the desire for security, the desire to be loved and desired, and the desire for recognition. He cites narratives of women and girls to illustrate these. These are people reaching out for some form of love and recognition, some kind of adventure, some form of solidity in the disintegrating world around them The failure to attain fulfillment of these desires can lead to behavior that is rejecting of the standards of society, says Thomas (1969). To quote him: "But we have only to refer to the criminal code to appreciate the variety of ways in which the wishes of the individual may conflict with the wishes of society" (p. 42).

It is Thomas's point in this book that prior to any self-determined act of the individual is a stage of "examination and deliberation." He refers to this as "the definition of the situation" (p. 42). It is not merely an act that is dependent on the definition of the situation, but that the entire personality evolves from such definitions, which are subjective and might have their roots in memories of past experiences, sometimes carried along in the nervous system. Therefore, interpretations will vary among actors and groups; and people and groups will frequently define situations differently, reacting according to these subjective definitions.

3. W.I. Thomas and the Unadjusted Girl

According to Thomas there is always a conflict between spontaneous definitions of the situation made by the individual member of society and those definitions that have been provided by the society. The individual leans toward self-pleasure, the society toward safety. Family and community have traditionally been powerful forces that have defined the situation for us. But with the erosion of both comes a greater emphasis on the individual.

As a social scientist, it is his position that understanding how situations are defined by individuals (or groups) is the only way an observer can come to a valid understanding of behavioral reactions and actions of the subject of investigation. This of course comes from his reading of Boas and cultural anthropology and perhaps from his reading of Weber and Mead. Thomas makes the point that girls are assigned definitions of situations by the societies in which they live and that more often than not operate against their basic desires and wishes as human beings. These definitions are not their own, but usually those of a patriarchy wherein a girl is assigned a particular place both sexually and morally.

However, definitions of sexuality and gender were undergoing enormous change in the first two decades of the twentieth century. As women poured into the cities from outlying rural areas and found employment in factories, department stores and offices, daughters of provincial immigrants rejected the norms of their strict upbringing.

It was clear by the early nineteenth century that the patriarchal family was experiencing a series of political and social challenges. Young women who were once expected to remain at home and under the protection and guidance of their fathers were moving out on their own in increasing numbers. As they did, many sought economic independence and sexual freedom. Newspapers, magazines and dime novels were frequently blamed for these challenges. The working girl heroine rapidly made her way into print and by the late nineteenth century she was frequently finding adventure, excitement, and love in the city (Denning, pp. 185–200).

Urban recreation and amusements often heightened sexual awareness. Dancing and social club activities permitted flirting, touching, and sometimes kissing (1989). New songs often contained suggestive lyrics. Going out with a boyfriend who treated was frequently the only way even a working woman could afford entertainment. And some women, referred to pejoratively as "charity girls" freely exchanged sexual favors for gifts, treats, and good times (Peiss 1989, p. 64).

83

Sexuality became a symbol of rebellion, but one that was frequently exploited. Many girls ran away from home from sexually abusive fathers or other family members. Once outside of the home they often used sex as a strategy for survival. Runaways often relied on boyfriends or men they met along the way to pay for their meals and hotel rooms (Odem 1996, p. 56). As these women gained autonomy, they frequently became vulnerable to forcible assault, yet the courts often looked on single girls as morally loose.

In his work Thomas attempts to better understand how these girls and women construct their own definitions, and how these definitions conflict with those that have been presented to them by their families and society. To do this he uses their unadulterated voices. Impressive about this work is the fact that these female voices are presented without much in the way of didactic editorializing. They are pure and resonant. They speak from positions of abuse, positions of helplessness, positions of heroism, positions of desire. These are voices of the "wild" girl, the unfulfilled housewife, the lesbian who must hide her desire for other women, the mother who abandons her children, the devoted wife who is sleeping with her husband's cousin, the unrepentant prostitute, the lonely adolescent girl who craves a boyfriend.

When this work was written, most social scientists felt that the so-called delinquent girl was the result of psychopathology, or some kind of personal deficiency. Thomas exploded this myth by presenting their personal stories and personal definitions as a mosaic of truths. We come to better understand and appreciate the great diversity inherent in the human community by having these women speak in their own voices.

In his introduction to the 1967 Harper Torchbooks edition of this work, Michael Parenti sees a similarity here between *The Unadjusted Girl* and Nathanael West's *Miss Lonelyhearts*, in terms of its poignancy and the sense of quiet desperation emerging from letters in the book (p. xxi). In *Noir Fiction* (2000) Paul Duncan cites *Miss Lonelyhearts* as a prime example of noir literature revealing the loneliness and alienation associated with urban America in the 1920s and early 1930s.

In 1929 West and his friend, S.J. Perelman, met with Susan Chester, who showed them some of the letters she received as a letters-from-the-lovelorn editor. While she thought they were funny, West saw them as heartrending and tragic (Duncan, pp. 32–33). He would eventually write a book that would become an American classic and reflect the times as much as Horace McCoy's *They Shoot Horses, Don't They?*

Thomas's ability to communicate the hope and desperation in so many different voices emanating from these disembodied women speaks to his talents as both a writer and a sociologist. Parenti, in his introduction to the book, notes, "In these pages, people cast about for new meanings—sometimes hopelessly, sometimes hopefully—as everything seems to be changing swiftly while too many things seem never to change, and no definition of the situation offers a final answer" (p. xxi).

In a nonjudgmental way, Thomas opens up a world to the reader that had seldom been visited except in imaginative fiction and the sensationalist press.

Conclusion

With his dismissal from the University of Chicago, Thomas was never to find a permanent place in academia again. While he and his wife returned to New York, where he secured a lectureship at the New School for Social Research and did some work with the Social Science Research Council, he could not easily pick up from where he left off. Ethel S. Drummer and other wealthy Chicagoans who supported him throughout the ordeal continued to do so. Drummer, a philanthropist and social reformer, helped to subsidize Thomas's research for the *Unadjusted Girl* as well as some later projects.

Amazingly, in 1926 the so-called Young Turks at the University of Chicago, under the leadership of Louis Wirth and with the backing of Robert Park, promoted Thomas for the presidency of the American Sociological Association. Despite the rigorous opposition to this move by some of the old guard Thomas won by a wide margin.

He continued lecturing, and did a short stint at Harvard. When his marriage with Harriet Park fell apart, he married in 1935 his research associate, Dorothy Swaine. She was thirty-six and he was seventy-two. Swaine became a major contributor to social research in the area of population studies. They authored a book together; and Thomas moved with Swaine to Berkeley where he went into semiretirement and she assumed a professorship. He died in 1946. Swaine herself would go on to become president of the American Sociological Association in 1952.

Sociology Noir

The story of W.I. Thomas is in some ways a modern tragedy. Thomas challenged moral traditions at a time when sexual revolution was in the air—threatening to undermine patriarchal society. His personal definition of acceptable sexual practices defied the standard proscriptions of the time, including those of his colleagues at the University of Chicago. Many officials of the university, including Small, Henderson, and Vincent (a new young hire), were all trained in the ministry. Although they were progressive on some social issues, they were not as open about human sexuality. Thomas stood out as someone who rejected the boundaries established by social tradition. He displayed a sense of disdain for established protocols and assumed an air of naive invulnerability. He appeared to spend much of his time moving away from his earlier prejudices and rural Southern upbringing. He fell in love with the city, with its dark corners and seedy taverns. Still, he was to become, as Morris Janowitz described him, a *bon vivant* (1966, p. xiii). He golfed every day, wore expensive clothing, and carried himself with conspicuous disregard for what others might think of him. Perhaps if he committed a sin at all it was this.

The Chicago *Tribune*, notorious for the red baiting tactics of its arch conservative owner, Colonel Robert R. McCormick, was relentless in its attacks on Thomas and his family. This was in keeping with its strong opposition to what it considered to be un–American teachings at the University of Chicago. McCormick was an important supporter of McCarthyism in the 1950s and of witch hunts that preceded Joseph McCarthy's rise to power.

Nevertheless, Thomas's work went on to influence succeeding generations of social theorists. The interactionist perspective owes its vitality to the energy he imbued in it nearly a century ago. It was Thomas, more than any other, who helped open the pathways for urban ethnographic research that tells a story and reaches into the heart. His specialization was urban *vérité*. His artistic renderings of the city and its people were made possible through what he called the *definition of the situation*. He used it like other writers and artists used their insights into their subjects—much like McCoy, Hammett and Chandler used their understanding of the mean streets.

Chapter 4

Nels Anderson and the Hobo

STRANGERS FASCINATE SOCIOLOGISTS. They hold a particularly important place in our understanding of who we are. Georg Simmel's classic essay imbues the stranger with both mystery and importance. For Simmel (1950), the stranger is an instrument of self-analysis, a catalyst for group identity who comes from places unknown to tell us about ourselves and sometimes leaves quietly but often stays.

There is a romance with the stranger, especially in our literature and art. Both hard-boiled fiction and urban sociology have made much use of the iconography of the vagabond and itinerant worker. There are deep secrets hidden within these dark figures, making them both exotic and dangerous. James Cain's 1934 novel *The Postman Always Rings Twice* tells the tale of a drifter, Frank Chambers, who is dropped from the back of a truck at a dilapidated roadside diner where he meets the owner's attractive wife, Cora. The two are immediately drawn to one another, and share their mutual sense of aloneness and discontent. They soon join forces in a plot to murder her husband, collect the insurance money, and make a life for themselves—*far away from this place.*

Being a stranger holds a very special position in noir fiction. There is sexual excitement in the loner who enters the frame to challenge the status quo—especially its suffocating domesticity. It is as though the vagabond carries with him or her some dream-inducing narcotic from the underworld which now gets injected violently into the veins of those living in quiet desperation—those waiting for something to happen.

The hobo as stranger and exile has long been an object of sociological allure. Part of this attraction has to do with the sociologist's fascination with personal marginality, social deviance, danger, and counter culture. This chapter sets out to contextualize the hobo and to offer an analysis of the University of Chicago study, conducted by Nels Anderson in 1923. It looks at Anderson's work as part of an intellectual and artistic endeavor to illuminate the lives of outcasts in the city in an effort to understand the broader social and sexual transformations taking place in society at the time.

Nels Anderson in his early years was a vagabond. He lived much of his life without a place to call home. He traveled the rails, found odd jobs in small towns and big cities. His associates were hobos, tramps, and bums. He slept in flophouses, in boxcars, and in cornfields under the stars. His life was a life of the itinerant worker—a hobo.

The hobo has a great tradition in the United States. Actually, the word hobo is thought to be the abbreviation for hoe-boy—the seasonal farmhand who worked the fields and traveled from place to place to do so. The hobo was the equivalent of an urban cowboy, riding the rails instead of the range. He never settled down—had no home. In Anderson's study we learn to distinguish the hobo, who works for a living, from the tramp who also travels but does not work, and the bum, who remains in one place and also refuses work.

Published in 1923, the same year as *The Unadjusted Girl*, Nels Anderson's *The Hobo* represents the first in the series of Chicago school monographs published by the University of Chicago Press under the supervision of Robert Park and Ernest Burgess. *The Hobo* was not only a masterful piece of scholarship, but it was also a book that resonated with the public, winning accolades and press attention.

Nels Anderson's Early Life

Nels Anderson was born in Chicago on July 31, 1889. His father was a Swedish immigrant who moved to the United States but almost never settled down. An orphan child of peasant stock, the senior Nels Anderson traveled across America finding occasional work and eking out a marginal existence. He married and raised a large family, which accompanied him in a covered wagon as he explored the opening American

frontier. His wife, Annie Witkinson Anderson, was American-born and
the daughter of Scottish parents. She gave birth to twelve children. Nels
was the second of these.

Nels Anderson reveals his biography in a set of narrative accounts
that appeared in book, journal, and magazine form (Anderson 1931; 1975;
1983). In 1906 he left home at the age of seventeen to pursue the life of
a hobo. In his story, he recounts having been inspired by dime novels
and also by the work of Jack London. Following in his older brother's
footsteps, he rode the rails and went from job to job.

> Above all, the hobo was a worker, one who moved from one kind of work
> to another when and as needed and who went his way when not needed.
> He displayed a way of appearing when and where new work was about to
> begin. He was an independent fellow who would leave any job if he felt
> conditions were unfair. Again, he would work six months or longer, then
> go with his stake to some city to "hole up for the winter," or to "rub off," or
> merely to "blow his pile." His next job might be in any direction or at any
> distance. Money gone, he did not shirk from "panhandling" (begging on
> the street) or from knocking on back doors for handouts. He was no walker
> from place to place, if freight trains were running [Anderson 1975, p. 1].

Inherent in Anderson's hobo narrative is a certain masculinity that
had an affinity not only to the dime novels he read but also to the hard-
boiled notion of the loner—the individualist who toiled on the margins
of society, someone who worked outside of the system and did not retreat
from violating the law should doing so be necessary for survival. The life
of Nels Anderson reads like an adventure tale. It is filled with the colorful language of a vagabond existence. And in a certain way, his writing—
and his life—bridge the gap between the frontier cowboy and the inner-city
bohemian.

He sold newspapers on the streets of Chicago, panhandled in Den-
ver, worked as a field hand, a skinner, a bridge snake, a miner, a lumber-
jack; he laid railroad tracks and served a stint as an iron worker. He stood
in breadlines, slept in flophouses and ate in soup kitchens. It was poverty
that drove him.

Anderson joined the legions forced into transience as the result of
the dire economic circumstances. He socialized in the hobo jungles and
tangled with the police and Pullman dicks. Eventually he was thrown off
a freight train moving through the Utah-Nevada borderlands—into a vast
openness stretching for miles. It was here where his life underwent what
he described as a "transforming experience."

Upon his expulsion from the train, at a depot called Crestline, he was literally chased away from the one-room station near the stationmaster's home. There was nothing around for miles. He walked a long distance in the hot sun and wandered into the nearby fields where he discovered a man atop a tractor. He stopped and asked the man for work. After a brief conversation, he was taken back to the rancher's home to a place called Clover Valley. This man turned out to be Lamond Woods, a Mormon who invited the young Anderson into his home for dinner. At dinner Anderson discovered that the rancher, his wife, and their children had never ventured more than several miles from home. They were fascinated by this young man's tales of adventure.

Woods hired Anderson as a ranch hand. He was given chores to do for his room and board at the ranch. Anderson describes Clover Valley as an oasis of communal unity. The people were endearing. Families gathered on Pioneer Day to celebrate and commemorate their Mormon-American heritage. There was a mystical quality to it all. There were potato sack races, baseball games, children and grandchildren mingling and playing with parents and grandparents. There was open-air music and dancing. It was an American pastoral tableau insulated from the seemingly deranged urban world.

Anderson lived with the Woods for several years and eventually went back to school, ending his hobo wanderings. He finished high school, joined the Mormon Church and attended Brigham Young University on a scholarship. He taught for a brief time in a local Mormon school. But his idyllic life was interrupted by World War I. He eventually joined the army and was sent to France where he witnessed much carnage.

Chicago and the War's End

Upon his release from the army in 1919, Nels Anderson returned to complete his degree at Brigham Young University in Utah. There he joined the debate team and became editor of the yearbook and president of his senior class. He developed close associations with other active students who had returned from the war. In a discussion with his debate coach, John Swenson, he was convinced to go to the University of Chicago to study sociology upon graduation. It was pointed out to him that his background and experiences could be of great value in that field. When he confided in his classmate LeRoy Cox, who shared with him his earlier interest of going to law school, Cox challenged him: "Law is a man's profession. What is sociology?" It was this challenge that convinced Anderson to pursue the switch to sociology (p. 157). He was now thirty years old. After a brief stint at high school teaching, he headed to Chicago.

Anderson returned to Chicago on a freight train. All he carried was his small bundle of belongings. He had little money in his pocket, but he was strongly motivated to attend the university. After exploring Madison Street, the area where he and his family had lived briefly side by side with tramps and prostitutes, he headed further downtown to discover the university he hoped to temporarily make his home. "The University of Chicago awed me," he notes, "those gray stone buildings, some with towers, the lawns, trees and walks. Few people were to be seen. Of course I asked questions about different buildings and saw myself being stared at, and for good reason, as I knew"(p. 160).

It was getting late, so Anderson sought out shelter for the evening. He spied the university's heating plant. This was a concrete building with a rounded roof and a large smoke stack. The structure, which was located mostly underground, was situated between two other university buildings. After filling up on coffee and sweet rolls at a nearby restaurant, he made his way back to the building. "When darkness came I went to the heating plant, spreading newspapers to lie on the concrete, and used my bundle for a pillow" (p. 160).

Anderson was now broke. He knew that in order to attend the university he would need a job. The next day he began exploring around the campus to find something he could do. His first attempt was in a building that bore a sign reading "Chicago Home for Incurables." While he thought that most university students would never seek work in such a place, he boldly went in to ask for employment. The director, Dr. Palmer, was an elderly soft-spoken man. Apologetically, he told Anderson that he never hired students, but that if he were looking for work he could recommend him as an assistant to the university groundskeeper, which he did. This allowed Anderson to rent a room near the university. From his roommate he discovered that his veteran status allowed him a tuition waiver. Shortly thereafter he was admitted to the university and was attending classes. There he developed a close association with Ernest Burgess, whom he found easy to talk to.

Burgess helped Anderson secure a position at the Home for Incurables after his groundskeeping job came to an end. He put in a good word for him with Palmer, who reluctantly offered Anderson a part-time position of male nurse in which he was responsible for helping to move and bathe patients and run errands for them. He was the first student to ever work there.

It was in Burgess's Social Problems class that a fellow student, a social worker, invited him to attend a lecture being given by Dr. Ben L. Reitman. Reitman was a social reformer and physician who specialized in treating patients from the underworld—hobos, prostitutes, tramps, and the like (Burns 1987). The talk he was giving was on the homeless in Chicago and Anderson described it later:

> Reitman was a man of middle years, attractive physique, about six feet, stout but still trim, big head with a bushy haircut, black mustache, and he wore a Windsor tie, then the symbol of some intellectual type. He wore a friendly, slightly devilish smile and he had a pleasing voice, but his talk was rambling, often turning in the middle of one sentence to start another. One might get the impression he was a sloppy thinker, but all the while he was getting over his ideas. Talking to social workers, he seemed bent on provoking them: they were always being outwitted by the hobos, tramps and bums [Anderson 1975, pp. 162–163].

Anderson stayed for questions and answers and offered his own observations on that population. Reitman listened with great attention, and then offered to take Anderson along with a few others who had stayed on afterward for coffee.

Discovering that Anderson was a sociology graduate student, Reitman discussed the possibility of conducting a study on the homeless in Chicago, and asked Anderson if he would consider helping him with the research. He intended to secure funding for the project from his many important contacts, but he asked the younger man to come up with some ideas for the study.

Reitman himself was an American icon. His work in Chicago among the homeless was legendary. Like Anderson, he was from an itinerant family—one constantly on the move. He sold newspapers in Chicago as a kid, ran errands for bartenders and prostitutes. He rode the rails in his earlier days. Unlike Anderson, he ran with a fast and dangerous crowd. He knew safecrackers and thieves, lived in hobo jungles, and worked a vast array of jobs (Burns 1987). After securing a medical degree he worked with the poor. He had been the lover of Emma Goldman as well as her promoter. He associated with radicals. Now he was a doctor to the destitute.

Anderson's second meeting took place at Reitman's office, located in a downtown skyscraper. Reitman assured Anderson that the money for the study had been pledged by a close friend of his, Dr. William Evans. Evans served as the head of Chicago's Public Health Department. Anderson would receive seventy-five dollars each month with an additional twenty dollars allocated for his research expenses. It would be funneled through Joel Hunter, Director of United Charities, Chicago's premier private social service agency.

Back at the University of Chicago, Burgess agreed to help oversee the research project but suggested that Reitman and Hunter join with him and serve on a small committee to monitor the work. They agreed, and now Anderson embarked upon his project. He rented a room in a run-down hotel on Halstead Street within the Madison Street area. It was located near an elevated train so Anderson would be able to travel back and forth to classes at the university and to his job at the hospital. The hotel was located in a place only blocks from where he had lived as a child (p. 165). His plan was to conduct a series of personal, informal interviews:

> Wisely or not, I began with informal interviews, sitting with a man on the curb, sitting in the lobby of a hotel or flophouse, going with someone for a cup of coffee with doughnuts or rolls. I had to develop some system in these interviews, as I had to devise some system in writing them down. It was not true, as some later assumed, I didn't "go down into the slum." I was at home in that area.... I did not need to be self-conscious in conversation with different types of men. I could talk without uneasiness as having come from one place or another in the West, or having done one kind of work or another. It was an advantage to be able to talk about the types of work men in that sector of society do, and work talk turned out to be a productive inducer to general conversation [p. 165].

It was Anderson's primary task to categorize the various types of homeless men living in the Madison area. This area is what he and others referred to as a "Main Stem," a principal city or area catering to hobos. Since it was difficult collecting data there, he relied almost exclusively on case method. He asked questions and listened carefully. His subjects could recount stories of a vast array of experiences and figures they had met along the roads. Over four hundred of the men he interviewed had credible work histories, illustrating how important the hobo was to the task of building the nation. Anderson took issue with the belief that homelessness was a sign of social pathology. "Their homelessness was seen as pathological in a society which assumes as axiomatic that every individual must belong somewhere, must have family, must have economic roots" (p. 168).

The loneliness of Anderson was evident in his inability or reluctance to develop close personal ties with his fellow students while at Chicago:

> Among the students there was a feeling that the world in which I moved was an underworld. They treated [me] as such. I didn't argue with them because I didn't want them to get to know too much about me. I was older, and most people were people with religious backgrounds. They were sons of missionaries, or missionaries, or the sons of preachers, or they were preachers. Most were religious, so that's why I had to be careful. I couldn't tell them that I was a bum at one time, or that I did different kinds of work, or rode the rails. All the time I was at Chicago I avoided women because I had no money to spend. And you can't have dates without spending. I was able to get through the year on my own earnings. I didn't go to dances, for example. Most of the time I was working on something [Personal interview with author, 1981, Toronto].

Anderson kept away from his classmates, and seemingly had some resentment toward them. "I had no friends. I didn't know those people at Chicago. I didn't want to know them. I didn't have the money to know them. I didn't have the time to follow them around" (Personal interview, 1981, Toronto).

It was as though the group of graduate students at Chicago was either aloof, or that he was very uncomfortable with them for a number of reasons. "There were a lot who wouldn't mix with me because they belonged to a different social strata" (Personal interview 1981, Toronto).

Anderson worked long into the night typing and transcribing interviews. He worked hard on his manuscript. After his first year he had completed two-thirds of his report. "I had material for a thousand pages," he noted, "too much for the committee. Much good stuff had to be left out" (Anderson 1975, p. 167). While the funding for the project was to last only one year, the committee found additional resources for another six weeks of work, saving him from ending the project penniless.

After submitting his report to Burgess, Anderson discovered that Robert Park had been given the work to read, liked it, and arranged for its publication through the University of Chicago Press. It was to become the first in a series of research studies on Chicago. While Park did some structural editing of the manuscript, he assured Anderson that it was excellent work. It was Park who gave the report the title, *The Hobo*. And in his preface to the book, he paints a portrait of the misunderstood vaga-bond: "The man whose restless disposition made him a pioneer on the frontier [and who became] a 'homeless man'—a hobo and a vagrant in the modern city (Anderson 1923, p. xxiii).

Hobo as an Icon of Marginalized Masculinity

The interest in hobos did not begin with Nels Anderson. Anderson merely made the hobo the subject of formal sociological investigation. The hobo had already become an important element in American liter-ature. The figure was popularized to some extent through the work of men like Jack London and John Dos Passos who themselves had been hobos. London, particularly, gave the hobo a proletarian cache as he joined with other unemployed drifters in the Industrial Army movement in the mid–1890s. In much of his hobo writings London helped to redefine masculinity, in a sense broadening its definition, by connecting it to socialism and American bohemianism. His autobiographical ren-derings of life on the road, his status as a social and economic outcast, his experiences as a hobo, spoke to the darkness and solitude of this exis-tence:

> I became a tramp, begging my way from door to door, wandering over the United States and sweating bloody sweats in slums and prisons....
>
> I was down in the cellar of society, down in the subterranean depths of misery about which it is neither nice nor proper to speak. I was in the pit, the abyss, the human cesspool, the shambles and charnel-house of our civi-lization. This is the part of the edifice of society that society chooses to ignore [London 1926, p. 86].

London would use his early experience to enhance his own literary appeal and bring to his reader an appreciation of the plight of alienated and marginalized men who struggled to survive against the harsh economic realities of the time. (Note the hard-boiled staccato of his prose.)

The journalist Joshua Flynt Willard did something similar in his book on hobo life, *Tramping with Tramps*, published in 1899, which was based in part on his own experiences as a hobo. Willard was born to a wealthy Chicago newspaper publisher, but after his father's death he was raised by his highly moralistic aunt, Frances Willard, who was a founder of the Women's Christian Temperance Union. He admittedly became a hobo as a reaction to what he viewed as a feminization of society (Flynt 1808, p. 44). Willard dropped out of college, road the rails with the common man, drank excessively, and made a name for himself as a writer of crime pulp fiction under the pseudonym Joshua Flynt. Like London, he combined his vagabond existence with a bohemian one—never leaving either far behind (Lindner 1996, pp. 115–117). Author, journalist, and amateur sociologist, Willard became the expert on hobo life prior to Anderson's arrival on the scene.

Rolf Lindner (1996) notes that Willard had studied sociology in Berlin under both Gustav Schmoller and Adolf Wagner in the early 1890s. Before Anderson, Willard developed an ethnographic approach to the study of hobo life based upon his familiarity with German urban scholarship and research. Still, Willard's style was in the great tradition of urban journalists. *Tramping with Tramps* was not a monograph, but a collection of journalistically inspired reports (p. 120).

In 1903 Willard penned *The Rise of Ruderick Clowd*, a crime novel about a second-story man driven by his poverty to a life of crime. This was Willard's second work of crime fiction. A close examination reveals many noir elements in the book. Willard's masked thief is a sympathetic character driven to disparate acts by social and economic circumstances. Like his hobo figures, the males in his other novels are hard-boiled; they are crusty on the outside with soft and sentimental centers.

Nels Anderson's study in many ways continued the hobo literary mystique. Like London and Willard, Anderson saw capitalism as responsible for many of the social problems confronting America. While he spends a considerable amount of space describing and classifying hobo jungles—the settlements, or camps in which these transient homeless could be found, little in Anderson's work shows the very dark side of jungle life. While he recognizes the drug and alcohol addiction among homeless men was a problem, his work in many ways sanitizes their lives. He gives hobos a respectability few ever actually acquired in a society that remained highly puritanical and exceedingly unsympathetic. He humanizes homeless men who were viewed as a blight on working class people. Of course, his definition of the hobo as a worker was not the only descriptor out there, nor did it have the most currency in characterizing hobo life.

For many the hobo was a petty thief, a pickpocket, a thug—one who was free from social or communal responsibilities, one who was perceived as a threat to the law-abiding citizen. For the most part, Allan Pinkerton's book, *Strikers, Communists, Tramps and Detectives*, published in 1878, portrayed those who rode the rails not only as unfortunate displaced workers, but also as scoundrels, potential criminals, and often political terrorists. Having himself been a political dissident in Scotland, Pinkerton now headed an agency that supplied private detectives to protect the richest railroads from the men and women who not only were too poor to buy a ticket, but who sometimes saw themselves as enemies of capitalism. While expressing sympathy for the docile "deserving poor," Pinkerton's men came down hard on those who tramped to survive.

Even if Pinkerton had some ambivalence for hobos, they universally despised him, as did workers everywhere. *My Father Was Killed by the Pinkerton Men* was a popular song in the late nineteenth century, sung with gusto in almost every industrial town where these agents served to oppress the poor and working class (Allsop 1967, p. 101). The word fink, which meant a strikebreaker, scab, stool pigeon, or industrial spy, is said to have derived from the word pink—a contraction for Pinkerton (p. 101).

As previously noted, Pinkerton himself became an author of early detective fiction, which in some respects was propaganda promoting the image of his Chicago-based agency and the agents who worked for him. Still, he is also a contributor to the noir currents that used the city's underworld as its backdrop.

Taking a page from Jack London, Anderson defends the hobo as the backbone of the transient labor force and the essence of rugged individualism. His now classic study begins with an analysis of the physical and social geography of an area he refers to as Chicago's hobohemia—a term he borrows from journalist Harry Beardsley, who worked for the Chicago *Daily News*. He neatly dissects the geography of the "stem" (a name given to an urban place where hobos congregate)—looking at specific streets and landmarks and describing those who lived in each area.

West Madison appeared to be the heart of urban hobo activity at the time. Here was the underbelly of the city, complete with drug dealers,

Sociology Noir

jack-rollers, pickpockets, and thugs. He describes the so-called slave market there where men sought out jobs in distant places while local ones
went wanting. He notes that one of the most striking characteristics of
this place was its almost complete absence of women and children. It was
most definitely "a man's street," he notes (Anderson 1923, p. 5). Nearby
is Jefferson Park, which became known as "Bum Park." "The town folks
of the neighborhood use the park, to a certain extent, but women and
children of the neighborhood are usually outnumbered by men of the
road, who monopolize the benches and crowd the shady places" (p. 6).

For Anderson, West Madison is home for bootleggers, dope peddlers,
jack-rollers, and gamblers. "The street has its share also of peddlers, beggars, cripples, and old, broken men; men worn out with the adventure
and vicissitudes of life on the road" (Anderson 1923, p. 5). The area
becomes the backdrop for many accounts of hobo life in the 1920s and
the depression-ridden 1930s. Frank O. Beck (2000, p. 35) was to write of
it: "In this great canyon stretching across the great west side from the
Lake, through the Loop and toward the setting sun, flow never-ceasing
streams of humanity, the largest number of homeless and hungry men
that have ever been brought together anywhere in our land." Hard-boiled
literature made much use of this place. Cass McCay, Nelson Algren's
innocent protagonist in his first proletarian novel, *Somebody in Boots*, lives
here for two months as he travels the rails:

> For two months Cass lived in Chicago in the fall of 1930. He walked up
> and down West Madison every day, one ragged bum among ten thousand
> ragged bums. He lived on what he could beg off the streets, and he went
> with a mind that was dark. Sometimes, for one day or one morning he had
> a friend, but only for one day or one morning. He was always half hungry;
> he slept in parks, he knew shame and cold. He was often afraid.
>
> Curled up on the editorial page of the *Evening American* one afternoon,
> within the lengthening shadow of some butcher-on-horseback statue, he
> wakened just as the sun was setting behind the city; when he brushed aside
> paper his eyes met the sunset, a thin red line between two darkening tow-
> ers.
>
> Lying here among other men now, staring and thirsting daily with other
> men, being part of this life led by so many other men Cass thought, in his
> moment of waking, that "Civilization" must mean a thing much like the
> mob that had threatened his father. For this too was a thing with a single
> mouth, this too mocked with pointing fingers. And as it threatened his
> father, so now it threatened him. Through hunger, cold, and shame it had
> pursued. "We have no work for you (he heard familiar voices); we have no

place for you. This is our world, loser. We do not claim you. You have no right here. We are *The Owners*. We Own All. Get out and get along, go somewhere else—keep moving till you die" [Algren 1935, p. 82–83].

Unlike Anderson, Algren peels back the skin to reveal the blood, veins, and sinus of urban life. It is the politically sensitive and sociologically informed artist like Algren, not the plodding social scientist, who makes West Madison come alive. In fact, *Somebody in Boots* was based upon some of Algren's own life experiences riding the rails, his own experiences on West Madison (Donohue 1964).

Like many of his contemporaries, Algren was both a journalist and a trained sociological observer. At one time he had intended to study sociology in graduate school, but instead he opted for a career as a reporter (Cappetti 1993, p. 157). His artistry in capturing the dark side of urban life set him above the many scholars and journalists who had also made Chicago their home.

On State Street, south of the Loop, hobos frequently had some money. According to Anderson, those with small change sometimes frequented burlesque shows where they could see scantily dressed women shimmy dance in dark smoky rooms. Also, there was an abundance of female barbers nearby, and Anderson is quick to point out that it was commonly believed that this is where women began to make their way into the hair-cutting profession—a profession previously closed to them. The hobos sometimes visited these women barbers for their inexpensive haircuts and shaves (Anderson 1923, p. 7). The class of transients here was certainly a step above those on West Madison. Cheap hotels abounded, and there were many here who took on small jobs to fill a void before they traveled on to something bigger. But this was before the Great Depression.

Anderson examines Clark Street below Chicago Avenue, wherein the hobo intelligentsia could be found. At Clark and Walton Streets, right across from the Newberry Library, was the so-called Bughouse Square, the place of hobo poets, writers, artists and revolutionaries. This is where hobohemia met bohemia. Men, again, monopolized the space of the park, exiling women and children to its edges. Here orators and their audiences gathered to speak of revolution or to ramble on about religion.

Bughouse Square was officially called Washington Square. It was the city's second oldest park, which had at one time been a cow pasture.

Beginning in the 1910s and late into the 1930s, Bughouse Square emerged not only as the best known free speech center in Chicago, but also as the best known outdoor place for radical oratory in the nation. It was here that the Wobblies, International Workers of the World or IWW, held sway.

Not far from here was the Dil Pickle Club. Founded by former Wobblies and soapboxers, the club was regarded as Chicago's premiere nightspot that served up food, coffee, tea, soft drinks, entertainment and radical thought. Opened in 1917 by Jack Jones (the husband of Elizabeth Gurley Flynn) on Locust Street and then at Number 18 Tooker Alley, the club became renowned as a central gathering place of poets, radicals, hobos, intellectuals, and artists. It was a generator of unconventional thought about politics, sex, and art.

The jungle deepened at Grant Park and Michigan Avenue. This was a place of rendezvous for boy tramps. But it became a gathering spot for many others. It was a hobo camp where clothes were washed and men went fishing in Lake Michigan. It was a place for lounging half-naked in the summer sun, and where camp fires roared during the winter months.

Anderson spends a chapter exploring the sex lives of homeless men. "Since most of them are unmarried, or living apart from their wives, their sex relations are naturally illicit" (p. 141). Anderson asserts "tramping is a man's game" and he wonders what it would be like if tramps traveled with wives and children like the gypsies do (p. 137). He believes that the absence of women on the road and the lack of females in the lives of these men makes a profound difference. It encourages a loner personality—men unwilling or unable to settle down for very long.

Hobos made frequent use of inexpensive prostitutes, and in so doing both passed on and contracted disease. However, Anderson emphasizes the frequent victimization of these men by such women. It is the prostitute who passes on the disease to the hobo, it is frequently she who rolls him for his money and then disappears into the night. Anderson sees these women as victimizers.

He then turns to the subject of homosexuality, which he confesses is widespread on the road. Citing Havelock Ellis, he suggests that there are two types of homosexual men, or "perverts," on the road: those who "differ temperamentally and physically from the rest of us [sic]" and are easily attracted by their own sex (often referred to as "inverts'), and those who because of the road are thrown in only with men and learn to substitute sex with boys for sex with women (p. 144).

All of Anderson's descriptions are of older men or "wolves" (later called "jockers") and younger men or "boys" (later called "punks") whom he sees as victims of debauchery. Nowhere in this chapter does he describe anything in the way of loving relations between two men, nor does he discuss male-to-male prostitution. There is also a built-in assumption that boys who ran away from home and took to the road were always heterosexual and were "made" gay on the road by older men. He presents cases of boys being seduced and kept by older males, and he even makes it a point to describe two incidents to the reader where he tried to step in and "rescue" the boy. His sentiments in this regard are little different from those of the Chicago Vice Commission, which he quotes. It was the commission's contention that homosexuality was a crime that was "enormously prevalent" and "growing" in Chicago (The Vice Commission of Chicago, 1970, 296). The commission called for this "crime against nature" to be better defined and controlled. By the late 1920s, the tabloid press was titillating readers with stories of homosexual child molesters who committed acts of unspeakable depravity (Kimmel, 1996, p. 204).

We know from Roger Burns's work (1980) on hobos that homosexuality was more common in the jungles than frequently thought. So-called jockers and punks filled hobo camps and most male flophouses. Sometimes these older men held on to their boys as if they were concubines or slaves. This was quite common among yeggs, or criminal types. At yegg camps, or jungles, jocker-punk relations were the most notorious (Burns 1980, p. 94). Here, some homosexual men carried women's names, and a few even dressed like women. There was indeed a transgender hobo population during this time.

In the 1890s the term "gay-cat" was applied to male homosexuals who tramped (Kusmer 2002, p. 140). And it has been conjectured that this is the origin of the term "gay" (Monkkonen 1984, p. 14). However, if we look at Jack London's use of this term in his work on hobos, a gay-cat was a greenhorn, sometime a punk, but always someone new to the transient life (London 1902, pp. 541–544). Anderson is cited as being one of the first authors to document the term "fag" as a hobo descriptor for gay men (Anderson 1923, p. 103). While the etymology of hobo language is problematic, there is significant evidence of the extensiveness of homosexual relations, and an ample interpretation of the hobo experience as, to some degree, homoerotic. Men lived together without the presence of women, and developed a degree of intimacy with one another alien to relationships in the business world. It was not unusual for men to sleep physically close to each other just to keep their bodies warm in winter.

Homosexuality becomes central to the lives of men alone, according to Anderson. But he sees it more as a matter of convenience than one of preference. While Anderson gets into some detail about why men have taken to the road, he never suggests that domestic sexual or physical abuse were ever reasons for adolescent boys to run away from home; nor does he suggest that some boys were cast out after a discovery of their homosexuality. There are no boys who use sex on the road to gain the protection of older males. By Anderson and others assuming that all runaway boys were heterosexual and were forced into homosexuality, he and they are able to avoid the threatening notion that the road was filled with men who desired sex with other men. He works to promote the notion of the hobo as the rugged male in search of adventure, or forced to leave home because of dire poverty. It was his assertion that the overwhelming majority of homosexual males, or "perverts," who rode boxcars found boys a practical substitute for women. Nothing more.

Anderson failed to see that Chicago's main stem, particularly the hobohemia of West Madison, "overlapped with that subculture of urban bachelors whose preferences for male company included sex" (Depastino 2003, p. 85). Main stem districts across the country were nodes of homosexual activity. Male prostitutes as well as female prostitutes were available here. "Like hobohemia, the gay world drew upon the cultural and neighborhood associations of the working class, operating through networks of cafeterias, poolrooms, saloons, theaters, social clubs, parks, baths, and rooming and lodging houses" (p. 85).

Also missing in Anderson's presentation is the extent of violence committed against gay males. Like the prostitutes, gay men were always portrayed as the victimizers and never as the victims. In part, this violence against homosexual men underscored the drive for a new hypermasculinity described by George Chauncy (1994):

> The attack on women's influence on American culture led to an attack on men who seemed to have accepted that influence by becoming "overly civilized," and men who did not do their part to uphold the manly ideal were subject to growing ridicule.... By the late nineteenth century, middle class men began to define themselves more centrally on the basis of their differ-

4. Nels Anderson and the Hobo

ence from women. As historian John Higham has noted, *sissy*, *pussy-foot*, and other gender-based terms of derision became increasingly prominent in late nineteenth century American culture, as men began to define themselves in opposition to all that was "soft" and womanlike [pp. 114–115].

Masculinity was not so much determined by the heterosexual conquest of women, but by an array of traits specifically associated with male activity. Maleness was often played out in life on the road—often in the savagery of hobo jungles far away from feminine influences. Chauncy makes the point that the overly civilized male "established the context for the emergence of the fairy as the primary pejorative category against which male normativity was measured" (p. 115).

Masculinity is critically important for Anderson. And this is evidenced in his portrayal of manhood in the guise of hobos, tramps, and bums. The hobo stands as the antithesis of the refined office worker who comes to dominate modern industry in the early 1920s. It is also a rejection of the middle class consumerism, and middle class womanhood. The road is the place to which real men retreat in the face of the feminization of work. Riding the rails, logging, wearing grimy clothing and having dirty hands are all trademarks of the isolated man:

When the tramp works he usually goes out on some job where there are no women. He may spend six months in a lumber camp and not see a woman during that time. He may work for a whole summer, along with hundreds like himself, and never meet a woman. Sometimes there are women on such jobs but they are generally the wives of the bosses and have no interest in the common worker.... The only company for such a man is men, and men who are living the same unnatural life as himself [Anderson 1923, pp. 139–140].

The Hobo is a masterpiece of sociological investigation as well as an important artifact of popular culture. It was a response to its time, and a salute to the disappearance of the male pioneer. *The Hobo* mirrored other works of contemporary literature and helped to inspire new work. Anderson filled the book with hobo incidents, with statistics, and descriptions of hobo types. He describes and discusses the missions, the soup kitchens, the clubs, the problems and politics of hobohemia—a city within a city. He provides the reader with hobo poems and songs. This was truly an important sociological venture into ethnography.

The ebbing of hobo life was reflected in Anderson's own biography. Here was a man who never comfortably fit into a safe, middle class world.

Once he had written the book and earned a degree of notoriety, he could not easily turn away and ride a freight train out of town. Still, as an itinerant scholar, he never turned away from bummery.

His skills as a researcher and writer won him positions with the Social Science Research Council in New York and a host of governmental projects wherein he focused on labor. He completed his PhD at New York University, and lectured at The New School for Social Research. He did some autobiographical writing and published in the *New Century*. Anderson went on to write *The Milk and Honey Route: A Handbook for Hobos*—a humorous work under the pseudonym of Dean Stiff—*Men on the Move*, a book about migrant labor, *The American Hobo: An Autobiography*, and *On Hobos and Homeless Men*, a compilation of essays and thoughts on homeless men. He wrote a masterful study of the Mormons, *Desert Saints*, which also deals with the themes of displacement and marginality, and wrote urban sociological textbooks.

Anderson's life took him around the world: to the Persian Gulf, India, Egypt, Britain, and Germany. Finally, he found a teaching post at the University of Newfoundland in 1963 and in 1966 settled into a position at the University of New Brunswick when he was well beyond retirement age.

Hard-boiled Men and Women of the Road

Masculinity was undergoing significant change in the 1920s. Men returning from the war often found themselves competing with women for jobs. The cities had grown up rapidly, and American culture was in transition. Office work was gradually replacing the city factories where men once had been employed in great numbers. Both men and women were attempting to find their way in a new social order.

Hard-boiled literature grew up in these times. The tabloid press was filled with tales of violence, perversion, and men on the bum. Tough guys were central to *Black Mask* and other conveyors of pulp fiction. With the rise of homosexual subcultures and socially liberated women, with the de-masculinization of work, heterosexual manhood appeared to be under siege. The tough guy image that was so central to this genre became a way of defining masculinity quite like the iconography of the cowboy of the previous century defined it then. This was an identity that resonated with the times. The male in exile, the male who lived at the margins of legitimate society, the stranger, had much in common with the hobo. In fact, in his analysis of tough men in detective fiction, Kingsley Widmer (1968, p. 3) suggests that the hard-boiled character is derived from hobo imagery of the 1920s. There was a certain ruggedness here, a go-it-alone attitude, a shabbiness in dress, a proletarian demeanor that could not be mistaken for anyone else. The cigarette dangling from the side of the mouth, the bruised felt hat, the terse derisive speech, the excessive reliance on alcohol and violence—these were all elements associated with hobo life. (p. 3). The hard-boiled hero is down and out, challenged by the society around him to fit in, but he refuses assimilation, or simply can't fit.

Hobo tales often excite the imagination. "Since parts of hoboing were in the tradition of romantic wondering," notes Widmer, "they furthered the 'masterless man,' individuality and scornful vitality of the vagabond adventurer" (p. 7). He also suggests that antecedents for the hard-boiled genre can be found in the lives and lifestyles of reporters, many of whom wandered the dark mean streets or traversed the surreal urban landscape in search of a story: "The creators of the tough guy and the proletarian hero were figuratively as well as literally the wandering reporters of the American scene" (p. 7).

Jack London, who earned a livelihood as a reporter, had earlier portrayed the adventure and excitement of the marginalized male just as the frontier was beginning to close. London's *The Road, Tramp Diaries,* and other hobo writings captured the imagination of a whole generation of proletarian rebels at the beginning of the twentieth century (Etulain 1979). His rejection of urbane conventions and his celebration of living close to nature with sole reliance on one's wits fired the imagination of many who took to the road. Those who were not challenged enough to leave took flights of fancy by escaping into his words. London's image of hard-edged masculinity helped to shape the popular culture of the day (Aurebach 1996, pp. 178–226).

Taken to another level of analysis, the hard-boiled male represents an aversion to women, and the need to "overcome a feminine 'outside'" (Forter 2000, p. 11). This tone in much hard-boiled fiction, replete with the cunning femme fatale or unfaithful wife driven by consumerism and whose sexual aim is to undermine and even emasculate the male and escape suffocating domesticity, has a corollary in hobo fiction.

Both women and men sought to escape from familial constraints and the repression of hearth and home. But women took to the rails in smaller numbers. And just as women who escaped into the city were seen as uncontrolled and of questionable virtue, the judgment was even harsher for those who took to the road.

One of the first hobo novels of the 1920s, Jim Tully's *Beggars of Life* (1924), was replete with hobo violence and women of questionable character. As in much early hobo literature, women were generally relegated to roles of hags or whores, or prostitutes with hearts of gold. *Beggars of Life* was an autobiographical novel (an enhanced tale based on Tully's seven years on the road) that laid much of the groundwork for hard-boiled fiction. Certainly it was a prototype for later works, and even influenced Algren's first novel. Tully, like Algren and London, cut his creative teeth as a newspaper reporter. In *Beggars of Life* his brusque dialogue, his hyper-masculine characters, and his disrespect for the accepted social standards became hallmarks of the noir genre:

> I lived in many a brothel where the dregs of life found shelter. I fraternized with human wrecks whose hands shook as if with palsy, with weaklings who cringed and whined at life, with degenerates and perverts, greasy and lousy, with dope fiends who would shoot needles of water into their arms to relieve the wild aching for an earthly Heaven. I learned the secrets of traitors and crawlers and other fakers.... Tramping in the wild and windy places, without money, food, or shelter, was better for me than supinely bowing to any conventional decree of fate [Tully 1924, p. 327].

Like London, Tully rejected the civilizing currents of modern life wherein people lost their humanity in the face of capitalistic imperatives. Having obviously read Anderson, he notes: "Neither am I interested in sociology among tramps. All writers of such drivel have not contributed one iota to the solution of the problem" (p. 335). H.L. Mencken, founder of *Black Mask*, published Tully's tramp stories in *Smart Set* and *The American Mercury*, which he also edited. Tully went on to Hollywood and had his best selling *Beggars of Life* made into a film that starred Wallace Beery. He wrote a series of other masculinist autobiographical works, and became a Hollywood journalist and publicist for Charlie Chaplin.

While Tully did not demonize women, he did marginalize them in much of his work. If we are looking for the origins of the femme fatale, however, we will not find them in his writings. But we do have the beginning of tough female hobos. Many women who road the rails, including some female characters in this work, could easily be mistaken for boys. In fact, to masquerade as a man was often a means out of a repressive dead-end life. As one student of hobo history observed:

> The number of female vagabonds may have been slightly underestimated because of the propensity of some women to masquerade as men. In 1880 the Railroad Gazette reported that one tramp captured by railroad police in New Jersey "turned out to be a woman in man's clothing." From time to time similar incidents of cross-dressing were noted in the press. Such a disguise helped women traveling alone to avoid the inevitable sexual advances that would have occurred had their identity been known. For others, however, taking on a masculine identity may have constituted a more serious rejection of the confining female roles of that era [Kusmer 2002, p. 141].

In his study of American vagabonds, historian Kenneth Kusmer recounts the tale of Jimmie McDonald, who in 1902 was leader of a notorious band of hobo marauders terrorizing farmers in New York's Monroe County. After the arrest, it was discovered that Jimmie was a woman, Teresa McDonald, a former actress who had escaped an abusive husband (p. 141).

Many of these women traveled alone, some traveled in pairs, others partnered with men, and a considerable number traveled in larger groups. While there has been significant discussion in the literature on hobo male sexuality, there has been considerably less written on the sexual experience of the female hobo. But historian Lynn Weiner (1984, p. 178) notes that many women who took to the road were in search of sexual freedom and an escape from the patriarchal family. "Most shocking to some observers," she notes, "perhaps, was the small group of 'lady lovers' on the road—the lesbians who tended to travel together and who occasionally grouped in communal lodgings in the cities." Women who rode the rails, lesbians or not, were often singled out for the toughest abuse by men, especially railroad detectives and police. In fact, many of the women who dressed as men were unwittingly breaking the law. It was not unheard of for a woman to be stripped by a bull and perhaps even raped (p. 176). It is important to note that the word "tramp" when applied to a woman meant something quite different than when it was applied to a man. Women of the road were seen as sexually "loose," and if they were alone they were quite vulnerable. Male tramps were seen primarily as n'er-do-wells.

Walter Reckless, another Chicago school sociologist, saw the rise in the number of female hobos in the 1930s as a challenge to male dominance of the transient life. It was the economic depression that appeared to force many more to the rails where they then competed with men. Accordingly, they began to "invade" this male domain "just as women have encroached upon all other original provinces of men"(Reckless 1934). Reckless saw this as a pathology in which gender norms underwent restructuring and women became more aggressive. But there were some who disagreed with this position.

Ben Reitman's *Sister of the Road: The Autobiography of Boxcar Bertha* (2002) presents an image of a powerful and liberated woman who road the rails. Published in 1937, the book combines Reitman's own experience on the road with that of his fictionalized female character, Bertha Thompson. While this character actually did not exist, the story's realism speaks to Reitman's close acquaintance with such people and the hobo jungles they frequented. Like much hard-boiled fiction, it is written as a first person narrative; it speaks of real life incidents and uses colloquial language. Unlike such fiction, this story is supplemented with charts and graphs on hobo life.

In the book, Bertha discusses female homosexuality on the road, abortions (performed by physicians like Reitman himself), and a host of sexual exploits. Accordingly, the author saw lesbians as relatively common. And many women on the road were bisexual. There were some women who traveled with gangs of men. "These were of the hard-boiled, bossy type, usually who had careless sex relations with anyone in the group, and who, therefore, never had to bother to hunt for food or shelter" (p. 49). The hard-boiled woman, therefore, frequently uses her sexuality to get what she wants. She is frequently cunning and dangerous.

Bertha Thompson is hard-boiled, but not in this sense. She is socially and politically savvy. She is no femme fatal. In fact there is little room for this type of woman in a boxcar. The highly fashionable, slender-legged femme fatal is driven by the ethos of capitalism. Not only does she possess a hidden lust for power but also a thirst for material things that will make her life more comfortable. This does not drive Bertha nor her proletarian hobo friends. Aside from a will to survive, she is driven by sex, desire, and wanderlust. She is a free spirit. Up until this time, it was commonly assumed that these elements drove only men.

Bertha believes in free love, and she does not use sex to manipulate men. However, she winds up working for a pimp and running with gangsters. Prostitution is a way of being closer to her lover. She is sometimes manipulated by the men she loves.

Reitman speaks through Bertha, presenting his views on hobo life—describing changes taking place in the community of vagabonds. Fiction is wedded to history as he explores the radical politics of that era, the rise of organized crime, and the corruption of the police and other public officials. Bertha is an outspoken socialist.

We learn that by the 1930s, many more hobos have taken to automobiles. Broken down Fords and pickup trucks are parked at hobo camps. We are told that more women seem to be thumbing rides on the country's highways. Bertha herself traveled both by train and automobile.

Sister of the Road is filled with positive references to counterculture institutions, such as the IWW, the Dil Pickle Club, and the Hobo College at Washington and Des Plaines streets in Chicago, which were frequently dominated by hobos. We are informed of lectures given there by Jim Tully, Nels Anderson, Ernest Burgess and a host of other Chicago school figures. "By far," says Bertha, "the most brilliant teachers and most inspiring speakers who taught at the College belonged to us and came from the life we knew" (p. 53).

Chicago's Towertown and New York's Greenwich Village were not only bohemian enclaves but also the locus of political and social misfits who found a place in the story of Boxcar Bertha. There gathered drug addicts, exotic dancers, writers, poets, gamblers, homosexuals, prostitutes, political radicals and killers rubbing elbows with one another.

While the book recounts the adventures and misadventures in the life of Bertha Thompson, including her love affair with her mother's boyfriend (a fiery anarchist), her life in prostitution and crime, her venereal diseases, her job as an assistant to an abortionist, her pregnancy and motherhood, we never feel sorry for her. She is a woman with few regrets and is a figure to be reckoned with. In fact, there are many strong female characters in the book. In contrast, the male characters in *Sister of the Road* are portrayed as relatively weak and ineffective—often eliciting pity in the reader. Bertha's philosophy of free love and her radical politics are all part of her homegrown feminism. There is far less plotting going on in the female inhabited boxcar than in the male dominated boardroom. But despite the presence of women in this dark marginalized space, it is still dominated by men—and by violence.

It is interesting to speculate on the relationship between the fictional

Bertha and other women (hobos and not) who might have influenced the author. Emma Goldman and Reitman had been together for a number of years before she was deported to Russia in 1917 for her radical political activities. One of the most celebrated anarchists of the early twentieth century, Goldman was hounded by federal agents for her incendiary speeches. Reitman had given up his medical practice among Chicago's hobos to follow her on an extended speaking tour. Barry Pateman of the Emma Goldman Archives wrote an afterword to the 2002 edition of the book in which he speculates that Bertha Thompson was "an amalgam of at least three women Ben knew." While Goldman was one another was a lover of Reitman named Retta Toble—a radical feminist-hobo from South Dakota (Reitman 2002, p. 203).

While Nels Anderson wrote about hobos right after World War I (when the depression had not yet deepened), by the mid to late 1930s there were many more people traveling across the country by rail and by automobile to find work—and many more women. John Steinbeck's *Grapes of Wrath*, published in 1939, chronicled the plight of Oklahoman dust bowl refugees who settled in camps in California.

The 1930s witnessed a good number of important writers who drew upon the dehumanizing elements of poverty to tell a distinctly American tale. Those who most contributed to the noir aesthetic related the story of urban marginalization and the ongoing struggles to survive.

Chicago's proletarian writers such as Nelson Algren, Jim Farrell and Richard Wright held no prisoners. Not only was their work filled with sociological insight, it also contained a degree of urban realism that had never before been seen. While their work is somewhat tangential to this subject, they most certainly were caught up in the currents of American radicalism that was epidemic in the Midwest at this time.

Hobo Noir: Down These Mean Tracks

Chicago's main stem became an inspiration for several hard-boiled writers. W.R. Burnett, who lived there and was a night clerk at a cheap hotel on West Madison, brought his familiarity with the seedy side of urban life to pulp fiction and eventually to the cinema. While working in the Northmere Hotel he encountered tramps, yeggs and low-lifes. He wrote *Little Caesar* in 1929, which was eventually made into a film starring

Edward G. Robinson—an actor who was to be forever associated with the American film noir classics. For this work Burnett landed a Hollywood writing job, moved from Chicago to Los Angeles, and in 1950 wrote the classic thriller, *The Asphalt Jungle.*

Burnett's work, like Hammett's, is deeply sociological. He constantly looks at the corrupting influence of the city on the lives of his characters. People struggle to maintain a sense of human dignity in their personal lives, but are drawn into crime not because of some innate pathological reason, but because of social circumstance and necessity. Still, greed, brutality, and treachery are portrayed as corroding human relations.

In many of his works, but particularly in *The Asphalt Jungle*, there is a striving in his central character to return to a bucolic existence, far away from urban desolation and wantonness. The Kentucky farm for Dix Hadley (played by Sterling Hayden) represents a lost paradise. After going broke from a bad wager, Hadley is forced to leave his horse farm, and takes up a transient existence. He is, in hobo terms, a yegg who throughout the story seeks an inner peace that is just out of reach. He sees his gambling and thievery as a way to win back the life he has lost. We understand that his last safe-cracking job is just a means to buy his way out of a life of crime. At least this is what he believes. "One of these days," he says to his female friend, Doll Conovan (Jean Hagen), "I'll make a real killing. Then I'm going to head for home. First thing I'm going to do when I get there is to take a bath in the creek and wash this city dirt off me." Dix Hadley's plight is not unusual. It is similar to that confronted by many men of the road. These are the people who left farms in large numbers to seek a livelihood wherever and however they could. Vulnerability rests at the core of these tough guys, but their exposure to the violence of their environs hardens them to the vicissitudes of urban life. They live by their wits.

Celebrity hard-boiled authors such as Dashiell Hammett and Raymond Chandler chronicled the dissolution of innocence. While their characters were often less on the margins than the hobos, they were most definitely inheritors of the tough-guy tradition. Like Anderson, both Hammett and Chandler saw action in World War I, and came home to a nation struggling with redefining gender and human sexuality, a nation grappling with an ambiguous sense of morality, and one torn by class issues. Much has been written on the deep paranoia that runs through their work. There is a strong sense of alienation and urban exile here.

111

Testosterone oozes from each frame in *Asphalt Jungle* (1950) with Sterling Hayden as loner Dix Hadley surrounded by James Whitmore, Louis Calhern, and Sam Jaffe. Based on a pulp novel by Chicago resident W.R. Burnett.

Hammett's first hard-boiled story, "Arson Plus," appears under the pseudonym of Peter Collinson in *Black Mask* in 1923—the same year Anderson's *The Hobo* was released. The name "Peter Collins" was hobo slang for a nobody. Thus Peter Collinson could be decoded as nobody's son. In this story he introduces a detective who would soon become known as the "Continental Op," or the Continental Insurance operative. This character was a composite of people Hammett got to know when he worked as an agent for the Pinkerton agency. The elements in this story—a middle-aged, overweight detective, a lucrative insurance policy, an attractive but dangerous young woman, a murder, and a twist in plot—became essential characteristics of much of the hard-boiled literature that would follow as well as the basic ingredients of early film noir. Soon Hammett would be writing for *Black Mask* under his own name and would gain a reputation for raising the standard for pulp fiction. His lengthier works, such as the *Maltese Falcon* and *The Thin Man*, were to make him a pop icon, and he moved to Hollywood in 1930.

Hammett's work, as well as the work of Raymond Chandler, which began appearing in *Black Mask* in the 1930s, represented the principia of American roman noir. Hammett and Chandler were inheritors of the hobo tradition; however, they brought with them a much broader level of cultural and literary sophistication.

Hard-boiled fiction of the 1920s and 1930s seemed to have been an important cultural response to the social upheavals that were taking place between the two World Wars, and a signal that the American frontier was now closed. The settings for many of these novels, and for the film adaptations following them, was urban Los Angeles—literally the end of the line.

Mike Davis (1992) has suggested that the Depression years, from which this new breed of literature grew, were marked by the virtual collapse of the upwardly mobile middle class and was underscored by a new type of cynicism unprecedented in American history. Much hard-boiled fiction came out of a powerful disappointment with the American dream. While the proletarian and hobo writers dealt with the bleakness of poverty and the promise of the open road as a means to escape it, Hammett and Chandler captured the essence of a depraved and faltering middle class stuck in a dark alleyway, a dead end, in the process of self-destructing.

Chicago school sociology of this era had much in common with noir fiction. Central to this approach was an emphasis on individual discontent and social pathology exemplified by social disorganization—an unraveling of traditional institutions. Unlike other social scientists who merely provided charts and graphs of summary statistics, Park and Burgess required that their students not only collect data but also examine the human condition in some dramatic way. Case studies in *The Hobo* and other monographs always include some subject biographies, and sometimes first-person narratives—episodes that lifted them out of the scientific indifference of sociology of the time. Take, for instance, the following excerpt from one of Anderson's interviews conducted near a flophouse run by Chicago's Bible Rescue Mission:

> I found a vacant place on the floor where I could have about two feet
> between myself and my nearest neighbor so I spread my newspaper and lay

down. I had more paper than I needed so I gave half to another man who was just circling about for a place to go to bed. I asked the man nearest me if the bugs bothered him much. He answered in the richest of Irish brogues that Hogan's bugs were sure efficient. Another man chimed in. He said they were better organized than the German army. How well organized they were I can't say but I was not long in learning that they were enterprising [Anderson 1923, p. 32].

Anderson was sure to use his familiarity with his subject to get personally close. Where it would have been difficult for an outsider to get the cooperation he did, he was able to get it through sharing his own experiences of the road with his subjects. Having had these experiences, he was significantly knowledgeable to ask the appropriate questions.

While *The Hobo* does not read like a novel, it does contain a constellation of human vignettes that add color and form to the otherwise uninspiring prose. The reader gains invaluable insights into what Anderson sees as a hobo "culture" and its changing role in American society. Anderson adds much to our knowledge and appreciation of the hobo as a person.

The overall success of hobo literature owed much to the work of the tabloid journalists whose colorful stories captured the proletarian imagination. Where the city had destroyed any real sense of community, casting people into lives of regimented tedium and artificiality, the people of hobo jungles sat around fires at night and exchanged tales of adventure and narrow escape. Journalists and pulp publishers appreciated how the public longed to be taken far away from the soul tethering monotony of factory and office life. The railroad and those who surreptitiously rode it symbolized a way out. It was a metaphor for rugged independence, and an escape to distant lands.

Social Realism

Hobo life was real. It was a reflection of the time, of an economy gone bust and of a growing cohort of the poor struggling to survive. If the locomotive represented the engine of capitalism, the hobo who rode the underbelly of the train was its unwanted passenger. However, as Anderson pointed out, without these migratory workers there would have never been a modern America.

4. Nels Anderson and the Hobo

In reading Anderson's *The Hobo*, it is important to appreciate the politics of life on the road. Hobos were not merely passive targets of abuse in cities through which they passed but were often outspoken advocates and agents for social change. When Nels Anderson surveyed the residents of Chicago's main stem in the early 1920s, only a small fraction of them had ever cast a ballot. The transient nature of hobo life meant that they were without a permanent address. Without such a residence they were unencumbered by social traditions and laws. The hobo possessed little in the way of property, with the exception of what he carried on his back. "He has nothing to lose and nothing to protect but his person, and that he protects by constantly moving" (Anderson 1923, p. 154). Anderson continues:

> The homeless man has no interest in common with the settled man of the community who has attachments to property, and at whose expense he often lives. The migratory worker, for a time, may be physically a part of a community, but he actually does not become absorbed into its social life. The wanderer who fails to win a place in the life of a community often takes his own course. This course is sometimes in harmony with the interests of the community, but more often is counter to them... [p. 154].

These people of the road were frequently the result of poverty created by the erratic fluctuations of market capitalism, and punitive policies directed against the poor. The Great Depression of 1893 was devastating to the working class and was one of the primary factors leading to the rapid growth in the number of migratory workers. While wanderlust may have been a factor driving some to the rails, the vast majority had no recourse but to seek their survival on the road and to eke out a living at the margins of society.

The proletarian nature of the hobo life helped shape hobo radicalism and anticapitalist sentiments. It put the hobo in constant conflict with the police and other symbols of bourgeois authority. The IWW, for the most part, was a creation of radical hobos living in Chicago's stem in 1905. "Chicago," notes Anderson, "has been favored by migratory radicals because it is a transportation center, and because of its tolerant attitude toward street speakers" (Anderson 1923, p. 230).

Unlike the more traditional labor unions of the day, this was totally at odds with the status quo, and not oriented toward grabbing a piece of the pie. It called for a revolutionary overthrow of the social and economic institutions that exploited working men and women. Every member of the IWW was expected to be a revolutionary, one who was dedicated to the overthrow of the system of capitalistic exploitation. To that end, every member was expected to be an agitator who made no attempt to organize workers, but rather worked to fan the flames of worker discontent wherever workers gathered. Members used Chicago as a training ground and recruiting center. From there its membership fanned across the nation, creating unrest and inspiring revolt wherever they went. According to Anderson, Chicago offered the IWW freedom for its activities not found in other cities around the nation at the time (p. 235).

Bughouse Square became a center for Wobbly activities and incendiary speeches for nearly every segment of displaced citizenry. Chicago's stem was not merely a place for hobos in the midst of migration, but an arena for the rise of a variety of countercultural movements that would influence generations to come. Certainly the radical politics of hobo life was centered not in an abstract utopian idealism, but in social realism. It was this realism that would make its way into the progressive art and literature of the time.

Conclusion

The contribution made by Nels Anderson to the study of hobo life, particularly his study of Chicago's hobohemia, was significant in several ways. First, it was a comprehensive sociological portrait. In doing this work, Anderson employed an ethnographic approach that is more concerned with the lives of people than the statistics which attempt to represent them. It was the very first in the series of sociological monographs published by the University of Chicago Press that attempted to bring attention to what Robert Park's department was doing. The Hobo signaled that academic research could be exciting and could take its place alongside art and literature in attempting to explore and explain the social world.

Anderson helped to strengthen the connections between the University of Chicago and the social service community. His work became popular and his findings were reported in the press. At the time, his vivid illustration of the drama of the everyday life of migratory workers brought needed public attention to the social problem of homelessness.

However, while he helped to strengthen the validity of ethnographic research in sociology, his venture into the marginal areas of the city, into its dark alleys and hobo jungles, put his reputation as a legitimate scholar at risk. He was never to find a full-time academic position in the United States. His appointment to the faculty at the University of Newfoundland in the fall of 1963 did not come until he was seventy-four years of age. He became a full professor at the University of New Brunswick in 1966. "The goal of my dreams forty years earlier," noted Anderson, "was not reached until ten years after active retirement" (Anderson 1975, p. 183).

After a first marriage to Hilda Buenemovitch that ended in divorce, but which gave him a son, Martin, Anderson remarried. His second wife was Helene Merchel. They were married in Penniac, New Jersey, on July 31, 1970. He was now eighty years old. Helene, who was a heavy smoker, died of lung cancer a few years later. Anderson retired from New Brunswick in 1974, but was subsequently named professor emeritus.

He lived the remaining years of his life alone in a one-bedroom apartment, just one block from the University of New Brunswick campus, and spent his final months in a local retirement home. He died in his sleep on October 8, 1987. He was ninety-seven years old (correspondence from Noel Iverson, 2004).

Chapter 5

Paul G. Cressey and the Taxi Dance Hall

THE TAXI DANCE HALL NARRATIVE occupies a significant place in American detective fiction of the 1920s and 1930s and in film noir of the succeeding two decades. The 1930s is often represented in film and fiction by the image of a dime-a-dance girl who has come to the city to seek her fortune but winds up morally compromised in order to pay her rent, selling her dances for ten cents to strangers on ill-lit dance floors in some seedy part of town.

This prototypical situation had great dramatic currency. The early years of the Great Depression revealed how the poor suffered under the burden of economic distress. The commercial dance hall was a new factory, an important service industry exploiting the problems of urban loneliness and poverty simultaneously. With so many alienated people ripe for manipulation, the chance to make money off the misery of others meant new opportunities for the criminal classes who often ran the dance hall establishments. The taxi dance hall came into existence at about the same time as the automat, only here men had their choice of women and dances rather than slices of cake and sandwiches. Instead of inserting coins into a slot and magically opening a small glass and steel hatch, which released the food, a ticket purchased from a person seated in a glass booth would be used to buy a dance (and perhaps bodily contact) from one's choice of attractive young women waiting to be selected. This was capitalism at its alienating best!

Pulp fiction and film noir made much out of this modernist phenomenon. The taxi dancer was central to the popular culture of the day. This character was prominent even in Cornell Woolrich's first novel, *Cover Charge*, published in 1926 (Nivins 1982). Woolrich's earliest hard-boiled novel, *Times Square*, which appeared in serial form between late 1928 and early 1929 in five issues of *Live Girl Stories* (a pulp magazine), involved a taxi dancer, but later his stories published in such hard-boiled magazines as *Dime Detective* and *Black Mask* contained several dance hall plots.

Woolrich's life was in many ways a tragic one. Born in 1906, he had hopes of becoming America's next F. Scott Fitzgerald sketching narratives of the Jazz Age. Falling upon hard times during the Depression, he turned instead to writing pulp fiction and is now considered a founder of American roman noir. He had great difficulty confronting both his own sexuality and the newly liberated women of his generation. His homosexuality was hidden most of his life and little in the way of its expression can be found in his literary work. Throughout much of his adult life he sought refuge from the world by living with his mother in a rundown hotel room in Harlem. When she died he lived with his aunt. Despite numerous brilliant stories, he found solace in alcohol and died a recluse in 1969, his more notable claim to fame having been the publication of his short story "Rear Window," which Alfred Hitchcock used as the basis of his 1954 film starring Jimmy Stewart and Grace Kelly.

Woolrich's portrayal of the taxi dancer was often associated with violence against vulnerable women, especially those of questionable moral repute. In one of his most important hard-boiled stories, "Ten Cents a Dance," the lead character, Ginger Allen, confronts a serial killer of taxi dancers. The killer stabs the dancers to death and continues to dance with their lifeless bodies, leaving dimes on their corpses when he departs.

While not involved in the production of the Hitchcock film, Woolrich did work on films for several big studios. Some of these contained dance hall women. Several films were based on his short stories, including *The Convicted* (1938), starring Rita Hayworth, *Street of Chance* (1942), with Burgess Meredith, *Black Angel* (1946), starring Peter Lorre, Dan Duryea, June Vincent and Broderick Crawford. In 1944 Robert Siodmak directed the noir classic, *Phantom Lady*, based on his short story. While the taxi dancer did not make an appearance in most of these, she was an important symbol of cultural change and sexual liberation not only in many of Woolrich's stories but also in the work of other writers such as Nevil Shute, whose *The Lonely Road* (1929) contained a taxi dancer as its central character. The taxi dancer easily made a transition from fiction to film.

As early as 1926, a silent classic, *Man Bait*, told the tale of a "hard-boiled gal" who, after losing her job as a retail sales clerk for aggressively fending off her male customers' advances, finds work as a taxi dancer. While dancing she meets and falls for the wealthy Jeff Stanford (played by Douglas Fairbanks, Jr.). The story is about love and the tension between the social classes. *The Taxi Dancer* (1927), starring a young Joan Crawford who plays a girl from the rural South in search of a dancing job, finds herself rescued from a taxi dance hall hoodlum by a cardsharp whom she helps to put on the straight and narrow.

In 1931 Lionel Barrymore directed a film entitled *Ten Cents a Dance*. This title was taken from a song written by Rogers and Hart, which had hit the charts a year earlier. Barbara Stanwyck (famed for her role in *Double Indemnity*) played the taxi dance hall girl who was romanced by a wealthy businessman and whose jealous husband worked to bring down his wife's admirer. The taxi dancer also made important appearances in film noir via John Huston, W.R. Burnett, Humphrey Bogart, and Ida Lupino, who played a hard-edged but vulnerable ex–dime-a-dance girl who became Bogart's love interest in the Warner Brother's production of *High Sierra* (1941).

During the 1920s and 1930s urban newspapers had been filled with stories of clashes between the police and dance hall operators. Police raids and forced closings were common. Complaints of indecent exposure and incidents of shootings, stabbings, and paid sex gave these establishments their unsavory reputations. Chicago social reformers such as Louise de Koven Bowen and Jessie Binford worked to close these places down. Even Jane Addams had referred to the dance hall as "a canker that the community must eradicate to save its future generations" (Dillon, 1912, p. 3).

The rage against commercial dance halls dates back to pre–World War I. Sensationalist pieces in the press, magazines, and books warned of the dangers of the dance hall menace, especially for parents who allowed their young daughters to leave home and find work in the city. The dance hall was viewed as connected to white slavery and a general fear was promoted that innocent young girls would be swept from the dance floor and made into sex slaves by devious foreigners (Dillon, 1912, pp. 7–14).

The scholarly interest in this phenomenon was reflected in the urban research of Park and Burgess and in their students who sought out the drama and excitement of Chicago's margins. Paul G. Cressey, the timid son of a conservative minister, found himself fascinated by the subject. Dancing was sternly prohibited in the Cressey home. And it was only when he went away to Oberlin College that he changed his own attitude. "My convictions upon dance gradually weakened, until at the end of my sophomore year I was willing to challenge the assumption that dancing was inherently evil" (EWB, Box 130, Series, IV, Folder 7).

Paul Goalby Cressey was born September 16, 1900, into a religious family in Franklin Grove, Illinois. His father, Roger F. Cressey, was a pastor with the Presbyterian Church and his mother Emma had come from a strict religious background. Cressey's younger sister, Lula, taught at a seminary in Godrey, Illinois. The Cressey family had moved several times, as the Reverend Cressey often relocated his ministry to serve congregations in various parts of Illinois and later in Erie, Pennsylvania.

Classmates at the University of Chicago remembered Paul G. Cressey as relatively withdrawn and quiet. He was small and dark (Faris, 1969, p. 259). He took several courses with Burgess, who in turn took him under his wing and helped him to secure a position with the Juvenile Protection Association. It was there that Cressey had access, as a worker, to case materials that helped lay the foundation for his own study of the taxi dance halls.

The city of Chicago was a bleak, crime infested place in 1923, when Cressey first came to study there. Burgess, who himself was curious about the dance halls, found in Cressey an eager student of loneliness and deviance. As he did with many of his other students, Burgess encouraged the young man to move into the streets with a pencil and notepad. He not only secured a salary for him at the Juvenile Protection Association, but also arranged for him to be paid, simultaneously, as a research assistant with the Local Community Research Committee which was also affiliated with the university and funded through Rockefeller Foundation monies. Burgess and Park had every expectation that this study would resonate with the urban culture of the time.

Dance Halls and Delinquent Girls

While much had been written in the popular press on the taxi dance hall of this era, very little in the way of scholarly research had been done up until Cressey's work. Still, the Juvenile Protection Association for which he worked was headed by Louise De Koven Bowen, who as early as 1911 had been a close associate of Jane Addams and a social reformer who saw public dance halls as harbingers of prostitution. It was Bowen and Jessie Binford, the executive directors of that organization, who helped raise the money to fund Cressey's study and provided him with much needed resources and background information.

The rate of so-called female delinquency had taken an upward turn in the first quarter of the twentieth century. Young women who lived alone in cities were no longer under strict parental supervision. Runaway girls who escaped sexual abuse at home, as well as young urban immigrants and migrants from impoverished rural backgrounds, sought out means to survive by coming to the metropolis. Others searched for excitement and adventure in the city—freedom from the domestic life sentence of womanhood. While tramping around the country finding odd jobs seemed to be more associated with males, moving into a rooming house and finding any paying job was more typically female. Since women were paid inferior salaries compared to those of men, many needed ways to supplement their incomes. "Dating" was often a means to do this. Connecting to men with money gave many young women a sense of security in a very insecure world. The men would frequently entertain young women and bestow "gifts" in hopes of some sexual return. Girls gradually saw a type of emancipation in their sexuality. But society fought to control this. However, there was great reluctance on the part of many reformers to see young women as any more than passive objects of abuse.

Since the term delinquency was coined it was almost exclusively associated with males. For instance, as late as 1955 Illinois state law defined the delinquent as follows:

> Any male child who while under the age of seventeen years ... violates any law of this State or is incorrigible, or knowingly associates with thieves, vicious or immoral persons, or without just cause and without consent of parents, guardian, or custodian absents itself from its home or place of

abode, or is growing up in idleness and crime; or knowingly frequents a house of ill-repute; or knowingly frequents any policy shop or place where any gaming device is operated; or frequents any saloon or dram shop where intoxicating liquors are sold; or patronizes or visits any public pool room or bucket shop; or wanders about the streets in the night without being on any lawful business or occupation; or habitually wanders about any railroad yards or tracks or jumps or attempts to jump onto any moving train; or enters any car or engine without lawful authority; or uses vile, obscene, vulgar, profane or indecent language in any public place or about any school house; or is guilty of indecent exposure; any child committing any of these acts herein mentioned shall be deemed a deviant child [Quoted in Burgess, 1955].

Young women could not be delinquents no matter how hard they tried. Much of the reformist concern about young women alone in the city was directed at their sexual exploitation by men (Alexander 1995). As previously mentioned, women who moved into cities by themselves were considered dangerously "adrift" without some form of legitimate male supervision (Meyerowitz 1988). The foundation of Victorian society, which held female chastity in highest esteem, was threatened by sexually active young women.

For some well educated progressive women of the early twentieth century, however, girls were not always innocent targets of lecherous men; rather, many young women who engaged in illicit sex were indeed "delinquents" in need of guidance and control (Odem 1995, p. 95). Sexual *looseness* among girls was viewed by some as an outcome of family breakdown, consumer capitalism, alcoholism, and rapid cultural transition in immigrant groups. Ernest Burgess noted:

> The urban way of life has freed the adolescent from family control and from surveillance by the community. This emancipation gives youth the opportunity for choice of interests, of career, and of a mate. But too often the choice is impulsive, irrational, and no longer dominated by parents but by the adolescent group [Burgess 1954, p. 158].

The dance hall symbolized the radical changes taking place in urban society—particularly in the area of urban commercial recreation. It was a natural outgrowth of the new consumerism. In this sense the dance hall was an essentially modern space.

By the early 1900s there already was a culture of working class dance halls. Some of these went by the misnomer of "dance school" or "dance academy," but these were meeting places that catered to young, detached urban workers. Early on, families were involved in neighborhood dances held in the rear of saloons or local social clubs. Large commercial ballrooms later gained recognition as meeting places for the young (McBee 2000, pp. 65–68). The local family-oriented dance venues remained popular throughout the first two decades of the twentieth century. For the most part these were ethnic establishments. However, traditional dances associated with specific cultures gave way, even in the homogeneous neighborhood dance venue, to more modern popular dancing that frequently incorporated sensual body movements, foreign rhythms and new musical strains such as jazz. The American dance hall was becoming a privatized erotic space with an admission fee.

Larger commercial dance halls gained in popularity with young working class men and women as they eventually sought to disengage themselves from the rigid social restrictions imposed by their parents and neighbors. These dance halls made meeting people who were not from one's immediate neighborhood much easier. In these new establishments, strangers could meet and develop an array of relationships with other strangers. Morality became a bit looser in commercial dance halls, and observers noted a certain type of overt physical intimacy that did not exist on the neighborhood level. Often well-to-do "slummers" would head out to one of these dance halls in search of erotic adventure. Frequently there was alcohol that lowered inhibitions.

Reformers found most of these commercial dance halls disreputable. Some drew their critical inspirations from other social reformers such as those in the temperance and anti-prostitution movements (Perry 1985). Most believed these halls to be the sign of moral degeneracy. The first two decades of the twentieth century saw the dance hall come under greater regulatory control. Restrictions were placed on age of female patrons, the types of dancing allowed, and the hours of operation. In these darkened dance places, police would often appear unexpectedly to prohibit certain types of dancing. Often policewomen or "matrons" would be stationed in dance halls to enforce the dance codes (McBee 2000, p. 71). Dance halls often hired their own dance supervisors to ensure that close dancing did not get out of hand. In Chicago the Juvenile Protective Association, under Jessie Binford's direction, furnished social workers to supervise these establishments and made regular reports on their findings (p. 71).

Taxi dance halls were a sub-grouping of this new commercial enterprise. In some ways they were similar to San Francisco's "49 dance halls," which were named for the Gold Rush of 1849. These establishments made money by having male customers purchase drinks for female employees who danced with them (Cressey 1932, p. 24). The women made their income from a commission on each drink sold. The taxi dance hall was also a unique rendition of the dance academy, wherein for a fee people learned to dance by being paired with professional dance instructors.

Girls who found themselves employed as taxi dancers came from different walks of life. Some were ex-waitresses, others former sales girls; some were Eastern and Southern European immigrants; others were refugees from the farm; still others were runaways from abusive situations, or just "incorrigibles." While selling dances was not the same as prostitution, it often became an avenue to prostitution or sexual promiscuity and for some a direct track to the underworld. Chicago's notorious Club Floridian on West Madison Street became a regular gathering spot for Al Capone's mob (NYT, May 3, 1931, "Bring in Capone Is Cermak's Order"). Girls found their sexuality to be an important tool for social survival. Women, especially poor women, were beginning to recognize their own value as sexual commodities. Physical attractiveness was of course the key to a decent income, as was personality. Working class media conveyed messages through advertisements as to what constituted physical attractiveness and fashionable clothing.

The Education of Paul Goalby Cressey

The Chicago school of sociology could not offer an individual like Cressey a better means for connecting to a world that fascinated him. However, the taxi dance hall as the object of his study was not solely his idea. Originally Cressey claimed to be more interested in a study of Filipino immigrant culture, and the taxi dance hall was but an accompanying interest (EBP, box 130, folder 5). In fact it was Cressey's hope that this volume would lead to a second one dealing with Filipino immigrants. Burgess thought otherwise.

Spurred on by Professor Burgess, Cressey continued his investigations into the "closed" dance halls—places that were open only to single men who purchased their dances. During this same period another graduate student at Chicago, Saul Alinsky, who eventually gained renown as a community organizer, likewise delved into the subject of taxi dance halls. This was also done for a course in social pathology with Burgess. Cressey's position as a worker with the Juvenile Protection Association gave him access to a wealth of materials collected by social reformers and law enforcement officials. However, as a social scientist he wanted to bring some degree of scientific objectivity to this work. He wanted to move this reportage away from the moralism and sensationalism of those who came before him. In this regard Cressey has been credited with significant innovations in qualitative sociology that helped give shape to the Chicago school (Bulmer, 1983; Dubin, 1983). It was his personal yet covert participation, his detailed observations, and his transcripts of encounters that made his work extraordinary. He "went native."

He danced with the girls, mingled with fellow patrons, and chatted with the owners, all the while using the vernacular of the day. His recordings of personal histories of dance hall regulars, in the language of the streets, reflected drama and pathos. It was the stuff of pulp fiction. Yet his facts were checked and double-checked before he committed them to his report (Bulmer, 1984, p. 184). Also, Cressey was one of the first sociologists at Chicago to recognize that his own unconscious drives, needs, and desires could and probably would color his reporting on his subjects (Dubin, 1983, p. 87). This is important to issues in contemporary fieldwork.

Cressey had a social psychological orientation; he was as much influenced by W. I. Thomas's work as were his classmates. Park and Burgess made every effort to instill in their students the importance of making the unfamiliar familiar. Certainly he drew upon Thomas's belief that "four wishes" drove most human action. Here desires for new experience, security, response and recognition played themselves out on the dance hall floor (Cressey, 1968 [1932], p. 33).

The metaphoric significance of the dance hall did not escape Cressey. He understood the loneliness that could characterize cities. He saw himself as a stranger to the urban world. Like those who were far away from home, or those reaching out for affection, or physical contact on the dance floor, he understood the isolation and emptiness that could characterize urban life. In this sense *The Taxi Dance Hall* was a work of descriptive art—just as much as Edward Hopper's alienated cityscapes. But it also had a hard edge. The closed dance hall was the scene of exploitation, commodification, and underworld dealings.

Cressey entered the dance halls, bought tickets and used the language of a participant. He was a client, a customer. He was frequently assisted by his fellow graduate students, including Philip Hauser, who eventually became a director of the U.S. Census and later director of the National Opinion Research Center. Hauser, who had taken the same social pathology course with Burgess, noted that he had done extensive fieldwork in the dance hall for Cressey, dancing and conversing with the young women (Bulmer, 1983, p. 100). While Cressey made no claim of exploring the dynamics of sex, gender, and deviance in his dance hall studies, his work was exceptional in this regard. One can see in *The Taxi Dance Hall*, in his detailed interviews and dialogue, the social conditions and social forces he was hoping to capture on paper. His interviews with the young dancers, with the women who worked in these establishments as well as their male customers, revealed both simplicity and dark cynicism. The transcripts of these interviews, which are housed in the papers of Ernest Burgess in the archives at the University of Chicago Library are dramatic and colorful vignettes. They are well worth the trip to Chicago as they capture a first hand rendering of the dance hall scene in the mid–1920s. But one comes away questioning how such intricate dialogue could have been transcribed word for word without the advent of small recording devices or overt note taking. Many of these transcripts had to be *recreations* of conversations. Just as there is recognition that Anderson's hobo interviews were not totally free from creative reinvention, the same must be said here no matter how impressed we are with Cressey's research. This might bring us to call into question just what Burgess was teaching his students to do. How aware were Park and Burgess that much of their students' research was but a creative rendering of the existing social world? Certainly, this imaginative embellishment was to be frequently found in tabloid media accounts. Were graduate students immune from exaggeration merely because they were social scientists?

Rolf Lindner (1990) observed that Park understood the need to make sociology more like human interest stories that could be found in the press and more like contemporary urban novels. It was certainly this struggle between the colorful narrative, do-gooder muckraking, and the dry statistical reporting that characterized early Chicago sociology. Eventually the dry laborious research model and the incoherent theoretical mumblings would win out in the academy as academics moved further and further away from the sensate world.

Portrait of a Taxi Dance Hall

The taxi dance hall had already gained popularity as a form of public recreation and as a subject of reformist concern long before Cressey began his study. Chicago was not the only city to witness a growth of the "closed" dance hall after World War I. Most large cities had them. He observed that New York City was the place in the United States where the dime a dance method first originated (Cressey 1932 [1968], p.181). One of the oldest taxi dance halls in New York was the Orpheum, which had opened in 1917 as the Wilson Dancing Academy. It was a place of noted celebrities. For instance, Allan Carlisle, grandson of Allan Pinkerton (founder of the Pinkerton Detective Agency), eloped with one of its dancers. And author Henry Miller fell in love with one of the taxi dancers he met there, June Edith Smith. He captured this meeting in his novel *Tropic of Capricorn* (Freeland 2006).

At Columbia University Arthur Lessner Smith conducted his master's thesis study on the dance hall in New York in 1925. Like Cressey, he focused on the closed dance hall. He also used reports from various reform and social welfare agencies in New York to draw some of his points. Though his thesis was only 45 typewritten pages, he included colorful remarks about dance halls recorded by investigators in their reports. However, his work lacked the depth and drama of his sociological successor.

What did Cressey actually find in the so-called closed dance halls? Though he found many things, he particularly discovered a heightened sense of loneliness and abandonment. This appeared to be a driving force that led men to seek physical connection with strangers. He also found oppressed young women and runaways from the lower classes, eking out an existence on the margins of the city. On the other hand, Burgess seemed to read into Cressey's work on the dance hall a growing demand for increased stimulation, including sexual thrills, a greater trend toward the commercialization of recreation, and the coming of greater sexual promiscuity. Perhaps both men were right.

Accurate accounts of taxi dance halls were rather limited in the 1920s. These were mostly dull reports of social reformers and the sensationalist pieces in the tabloids. But Cressey moved beyond this. *The Taxi Dance Hall* approached the topic with both scholarly professionalism and colorful depiction. Cressey's book begins with a sketch of the Eureka

Sociology Noir

Dancing Academy, a fictitiously named taxi dance hall located on the second floor of a deteriorating building located close to a central street-car intersection in Chicago. It is obviously nighttime: "Only a dully lighted electric sign flickering forth the words 'Dancing Academy,' a congregation of youths and taxicabs at the stairway entrance, and an occasional blare from a jazz orchestra within indicate to the passer-by that he is near one of Chicago's playgrounds" (Cressey 1968 [1932], p.4). On closer inspection of the place, however, one sees a crudely written portable sign reading, "Dancing Tonight! Fifty Beautiful Lady Instructors" (p. 4).

Cressey describes the arriving evening crowd. A motley group of patrons walking, stepping off the streetcars, driving up in automobiles, or arriving in taxicabs. For the most part these are men alone, or in groups of two or three. Some are rowdy boys. They are smoking cigarettes; a few are sleekly groomed. "Others are middle-aged men whose stooped shoulders and shambling gait speak eloquently of a life of manual toil" (p.4). Some are European immigrants who have little knowledge of English; many are young Filipino men. There are also recent rural migrants to Chicago among them.

Cressey then gives the reader a description of the girls' arrival. For the most part these young women are from the lowest social rank:

> They wear the same style of dress, daub their faces in the same way, chew their chicle in the same manner.... Some approach the entrance in a decorous manner, others with loud laughter, slang, and profanity. The girls most frequently alight from the street cars, sometimes alone, often in groups of two or three. Some of them live within walking distance.... Frequently an overflowing taxicab conveys three or four girls, accompanied by an equal number of men. The girls, trim in their fur coats and jauntily worn hats, hurry across the sidewalk, through the entrance and up the stairs... [p. 5].

The place itself is dark and impersonal. "In a narrow glass cage at the head of the stairs sits the ticket-seller, with immobile countenance. He indicates by a flicker of the eyelids and a glance toward the sign stating the admission fee that entrance will be granted upon the payment of a prescribed charge of $1.10. Stuffing into convenient pockets the long strip of dance tickets the patron is then ushered through the checkroom and into the main hall" (p. 6).

This is no bland narrative. Cressey captures the mood of the place, including that of the orchestra:

5. Paul G. Cressey and the Taxi Dance Hall

On a platform at one end of the hall the five musicians of the orchestra
wriggle, twist, and screech. But their best efforts to add pep and variety to
the monotonous "Baby Face, You've Got the Cutest Little Baby Face" win
no applause. The dancers are musically unappreciative, entirely oblivious to
the orgiastic behavior on the orchestra stand [p. 6].

There are some two hundred men in the room and very few of them
are dancing. "They stand about the edge of the dance space or slouch
down into the single row of chairs ranged along the wall and gaze fixedly
upon the performers. No one speaks. No one laughs. It is a strangely
silent crowd" (p. 6). Then after the music subsides, it begins anew and
the dance floor is crowded, becoming "a mass of seething, gesticulating
figures; sideline spectators dart hither and thither after girls of their choice,
while other men slump down into their vacated seats" (p. 6).

The women of the dance halls are most decidedly hard-boiled. "[They]
seek to enhance their attractiveness by every feminine device—rouge, lip-
stick, and fetching coiffures. Even the silken dress seems sometimes to
serve its mistress professionally. When business is dull the unchartered
girls frolic together over the floor, their skirts swish about, the side-line
spectators gape and reach for more tickets" (p. 7).

While most of these young women appear to be attractive, vivacious,
and slim, they "need not be thought of as virtuous." In fact there are
some who are a bit "more brazen than the rest" with "too generously
applied" rouge. Such a woman dances by with "cynically curled lips" and
in her dancing one can see a "revolt against the conventional" (p. 7).

Cressey makes much of social outcasts among the patrons. Aside
from the old, middle aged, and younger men there are "recent industrial
recruits from the country, eager to experience some of the thrills of city
life" (p. 10). There are also "footloose globe-trotters" and "hobo journey-
men." But there are many for whom this is perhaps their only chance of
meeting a women.

Finally, there are a few men, handicapped by physical disabilities, for whom
the taxi dancer's obligation to accept all comers makes the establishment a
haven of refuge. The dwarfed, maimed, and the pock-marked all find social
acceptance here; and together with the other variegated types they make the
institution a picturesque and rather pathetic revelation of human nature
and city life [p. 10].

Cressey sees in the dance hall a cross section of American urban
life. The dancers, patrons and managers constitute a composite of the

lower rungs of urban society. While his opening chapter is a descriptive overview, which breaks down the dance hall into a respective typology (i.e., discussion of differences between the dance pavilion, the roadhouse, the cabaret, the dance academy and so on), subsequent ones deal with the sociological significance of the phenomenon.

Deviance and the Dance Hall

For Cressey, while it is obvious that it dwells at the urban margins, the taxi dance hall is also a mechanism for integrating alienated urban life. In a series of transcripts of his dance hall interviews, he gives the reader a dramatic rendering of the dancers' lives. Using the vernacular of the street, Cressey comes to be at home with those who dwell at the edges of the city. In this sense his portrait of the taxi dancer, her employer, and her patron is a work of modernism—much in the same sense as the occasional dime novel these people sometimes read. On some level it broaches the sensibilities of Toulouse-Lautrec in that it is a vivid and colorful portrayal of urban profligacy. Cressey neither romanticized nor demonized those he interviewed, but attempted to accurately portray their lives, their desires, their biases, their dreams.

Though the family backgrounds of the taxi dance hall girls vary, it appears as though most were escaping poverty or familial distress. Though most were from the city of Chicago, a good number were from the rural outskirts or other cities; and some were immigrants from Sweden, France, Germany, and elsewhere. Cressey carefully mapped where each girl he had spoken to lived in the city, and concluded that the taxi dancer was "considerably detached from her early neighborhood ties" (Cressey, p. 57). The majority of the Chicago girls, however, appeared to come originally from the Polish, Jewish, and Italian sections of the city (p. 58). In at least two thirds of his sample, fathers who were then the primary economic support were absent from the girls' homes. But even those homes with residing fathers were problematic. Aside from intergenerational and cultural clashes over values and dress he also found a significant pattern of psychological disturbance in some of these girls' homes (p. 63). Many of the girls who remained living at home kept their lives as taxi dancers secret, and lied about what they did (p. 75).

In no way does Cressey give the reader the impression that these girls were all innocent victims, or that they were somehow inherently bad. As a sociologist he attempts to show just how life circumstances led some of these young women to seek refuge and security at the dance hall. He stresses the addictive nature of such a life—one characterized by sexual excitement and money—a community of its own in which the young woman often finds "a substitute for the inadequacy of her home" (p. 82).

Alma, a sixteen-year-old girl Cressey interviewed, tells a story of being forced to quit school at age 14 to go to work to help support the family—a mother and ten children. Her father, a farmer, died of pleurisy when she started high school; her mother went on home relief and eventually entered a life of prostitution in Marshfield, Wisconsin. Her younger sister soon followed her mother into this life:

> We were all raised Lutherans. My father was a Lutheran but my mother was nothing. When we moved to Marshfield, the children were divided. We two oldest girls married, the second boy, Robert, was sent to reform school. He was born at eight months pregnancy and was small and mean. He even tried to kill me once by aiming a hatchet at my head. I stood my ground and dared him to try. Two of the younger children are in the Children's Home and two adopted out.
>
> I have been on my own ever since I was nine years old. I was bright in school and always wanted to go on. I did all kinds of things to earn my way through school. I worked in people's homes and after school, worked as a waitress in a restaurant and helped at harvesting times and once helped to feed twenty-seven people each day for three weeks. I even worked around the binders and shellers. I would stay on in school but my mother tried to get me to give up school and come and be with her as a prostitute [EBP box 130, folder 5].

In this transcript, Alma continues her tale of an early marriage "in order to keep from being a prostitute." She tells a story of pregnancy, physical abuse by her new husband and rejection by him. She recounts his affair with her girlfriend who eventually moves in with them. She begins drinking and takes up smoking to numb herself. Soon thereafter Alma departs for Chicago, leaving her new baby and husband behind.

She arrives in the city with $1.50 in her purse and no one she can call on for help. "After I got here I got to worry about my troubles. I planned to commit suicide twice. The first time I tried to borrow a revolver from my landlady but she got me when I tried to make it to my room. Of course I had to leave." Her second attempt was a jump into Lake Michigan, but she was stopped by a sailor before she had the chance.

While working at the Drop In Restaurant at Clark and Van Buren, Alma was approached by a dance hall manager who offered her a job as a taxi dancer at the Chicago Dance Academy (a fictitiously named establishment). It was a place to make money and she claimed to make thirty dollars a week. "I don't go to the hall to make friends. I go there to make money." She continues:

> Everybody says I look happy and peppy but usually I feel just the opposite but I know I couldn't show my real feelings or I don't get the dances.
>
> It pays to dance close and fast but not to shake it up. I don't have to shake it up to get all the dances I want, but I have a good form and always wear my dresses to show my shape. It's just a question of making the most of what you've got to work at. All I got to work with is "sex appeal" [p. 48].

Alma relates her dance hall exploits to the interviewer: "The first thing to being a successful gold digger is to choose the right fellow." She continues:

> The first impression that a girl has to make is that she is a good girl, under hard circumstances. Then when a fellow asks for a date she tells him how hard up she is and she would like to go out but that she needs the money and has to come to the hall and work every night. Then get the idea across to him that I'll go with him, if he'll pay me what I'd make if I stayed in the hall that night. When he asks how much that is I make it seven or eight dollars rather than $4 which it usually is. I always insist on getting the money before I go out then they take me to a café and after I gotten a good meal off of him, I invent some way of getting away. One way is to ask to be excused having meant either to a telephone or to a restroom and then I go out another door and ditch him....

Alma tells the interviewer how she met a man with whom she's planning to establish a dance act. She's hoping to go on tour with him: "I got a few good friends here in the city now and when I'm a good friend I'm a good friend and not a fair weather friend. Of course I have to ___the men some but I don't ___my friends." She ends the interview on a philosophical note:

> There ain't any hell any way. I figure all the hell one has is right here. Your heavens are here too, but I never found very many. It's a shame a girl can't go straight and have a good time but I've got to get what I get by "sex appeal." There's one advantage I've got now, the men can't work me up and so I'm safe.

Alma's tale reflects the central noir elements including the dark pessimism, shallowness and sometimes racism associated with the white working class poor. This is evident in her final confidence to her interviewer: "I like the Chicago because there ain't any Filipinos there. They make me sick. I won't dance with them."

Race and Sex at the Dance Hall

The issue of race has an important role in the dance halls of Chicago, almost as significant as sex. Cressey saw this as a central area of his research interest. He observed that many of the patrons at various dance halls were male immigrants from the Philippines.

Chicago had been the scene of an influx of Filipino immigrants following the Spanish-American War. It was then that the U.S. enacted policies to invite the children of elites from abroad to study American culture and teach them English for the purpose of better incorporating these elites into the colonial system. *Pensionados*, men given state scholarships to study in the United States, became more common. Chicago was a place where many of these detached young men from well-to-do families came to study. The census data reveal a growth in the Filipino population in the city from 3 in 1910 to 154 in 1920 to 1,796 by 1930. The vast majority of these were males living away from their homeland who had intentions of returning to the Philippines (Posadas and Guyotte, 1990). Nevertheless, many of them settled into Chicago working at service jobs such as waiter, dishwasher, porter and bellboy, in statuses well below their educational accomplishments.

In California, where most Filipino migrants were unskilled farmhands of the lower classes, racial barriers were imposed that prohibited Filipinos from marrying or even dating white women (Parrenas, 1998). However, the taxi dance hall had become a beacon of racial mixing. It was a place where Filipino men could dance with white women for the price of a ticket. This has led anthropologist Rachel Salazar Parrenas (1998) to consider at least some of the vehement pressures on authorities to close taxi dance halls as guided by racism (p. 116).

Racial mingling challenged the existing American apartheid and the racial purity of American womanhood. However, in the west the influx of Filipino wage earners was an added pressure. Despite the fact that many reformers viewed the dance hall as a cauldron of immorality, the need to keep the race pure was a national priority in the first two decades of the twentieth century, which saw an upswing in the power of the Klu Klux Klan. In taxi dance halls generally, black men were excluded admission, except as band members; however, Filipinos, often referred to as "little brown monkeys," found some degree of acceptance. According to Cressey, this happened in Chicago because one central dance hall proprietor had roomed with Filipino college students in Detroit and liked them (Cressey, p. 197).

The scarcity of Filipino women, local antimiscegenation laws (particularly adopted in the western states in the early 1930s), and the blatant racism forced Filipino men into bachelorhood (Parrenas 1998). A major riot took place at a taxi dance hall in Watsonville, California, in 1930 where male Filipino farm workers danced with white women (Maira 2000). Whites attacked a taxi dance hall, killing at least one Filipino. While racism also existed in Chicago, its primary target was blacks migrating from the South and not Asians, as was the case on the West Coast. While "black and tan" cabarets that existed in the black belt welcomed black-white mingling, this was not the case in the Chicago dance halls (Cressey, p. 44). In these establishments Filipinos were good customers. A significant number of them were college students or college educated.

Cressey estimated that at least a fifth of the total patrons of Chicago's taxi dance halls were Filipinos (p. 145). It was Cressey's contention that the taxi dance hall played an important role in acclimating Filipino men to American life (p. 152):

> It provides him with his first opportunity for social contacts with American young women. Even though still diffident and uncertain of himself, he may, with his tickets, buy an unchallenged claim to a young woman's society and attention for at least a brief period. It is, in a sense, a 'school' by which he gains self-confidence and a certain degree of social ease when among white Americans. It likewise provides him with the thrills and novelties which he anticipates [pp. 152–153].

Cressey points out that taxi dance halls existed in the Philippines, but these were designated "cabarets." The dance hall in America was thus a familiar kind of place to many émigrés. But even in the Philippines the taxi dance hall girls (*bailarinas*) were of a lower social class than the young male students who would frequent the clubs. It was unlikely that any serious relationship between these men and women would materialize there.

Still, it was the coming into physical contact with white American women for the first time that provided the Filipino patron with both a sense of acceptance and excitement:

> Just to have a date with an American girl, and to be alone with her in a taxicab, and perhaps to kiss her, is enough for a time for most Filipinos. I'll always remember my first date with an American girl. She was a dance-hall girl, but I thought she was wonderful. We were alone together in a taxicab and later I took her to a chop-suey restaurant. I didn't dare to do more than hold her hand, but I had a wonderful time [pp. 153–154].

While Rachael Parrenas (1998) attempts to show how gender alliances formed between white taxi dance hall women and Filipino immigrant men in the 1920s and 1930s, Cressey's research does not bear this out—especially in Chicago. Cressey implies that most relationships between Filipino men and white women of the taxi dance hall were ones of convenience at best and mutual exploitation at worse. Despite a relatively small number of interracial marriages among these groups, many of these ended in divorce. In fact Cressey found considerable racism among the taxi dancers in Chicago, even among those who married Filipinos (Cressey, pp. 167–174). "Oh, these Niggers [Filipinos] and Chinks [Chinese] are just fish to the girls," says one taxi dancer's white boyfriend. "The girls keep them on a string for what they can get out of them" (Cressey, p. 44).

One taxi dancer remarks: "The 'Flips' [Filipinos] are all right for anybody that wants them. They're a lot more polite than most of the other fellows who come up here. But they're not white, that's all. Of course I'll dance with them at the hall. But I won't go out with them. I'm white and I intend to stay white" (Cressey, p. 44).

The Changing Moral Landscape

The impact of the taxi dance hall on the sexual landscape of the city was palpable. Restrictive moral codes and local decency laws that attempted to keep the taxi dance halls in check were constantly challenged in the lower courts. While it was not unusual for Chicago police to raid a dance hall and arrest the women for indecent attire, or revoke the license of the establishment, judges frequently dismissed these cases. In one such instance police closed a dance hall for girls wearing short skirts and no stockings:

The fact that the majority of girls who visited the hall in the summer did not wear stockings is not sufficient proof to substantiate a charge of indecent exposure," Judge Lindsay ruled. "If the police exercised their visual powers they might have seen hundreds of women minus such garb on Chicago streets. As to the abbreviated skirts, I again call attention to the style of dress common on the streets, in homes, and the most fashionable ballrooms of the city.... Although this court is not primarily interested in sartorial niceties, or in defense of fickle fashion, it cannot but condemn the tinge of the strained saintliness in the attitude of the police [CDT, October 16, 1929, p. 5].

While the courts frequently upheld the rights of taxi dance halls to exist and issued injunctions against the police, by the early 1930s organized crime had begun to control a number of these establishments in and around Chicago. The public clamor for their closing grew louder as shootings and bombings and racial conflicts intensified. Self-policing practices of many dance halls degenerated as young women more frequently launched lives of prostitution from these facilities.

The Colonial, a sister dance hall to Al Capone's Club Floridian, held regular costume parties wherein the women were dressed in nothing but brassieres, shorts, and slippers (CDT, April 21, 1932, p. 1). Frequently racial skirmishes and gang violence broke out. These were different places than the ones examined by Cressey in 1927.

The mayor, the press, and the police delivered all-out attacks against these establishments and were urged on by social reform organizations. The city's Corporation Counsel that prosecuted these establishments saw at least eleven of the dance halls under the control of the syndicate (CDT April 24, 1932, p. 13).

Cressey, however, found himself defending these dance halls from their patriarchal accusers even though the agency with which he worked (the Juvenile Protection Association) demanded their closure. He seemed to understand that the attacks against these establishments were often motivated by an attempt to keep young women from establishing lives of their own, to keep them from using their sexuality as a form of power over men. Dance halls appeared to be on the forefront of cultural change, places where casual sex became more commonplace. However, in keeping with the currents of his time, Cressey saw these establishments as contributing to the personal demoralization of some. Still he recognized their importance for providing outlets for those who needed such places in their lives—for the women and men who might have found themselves in much worse positions without the dance hall (Cressey, 282).

When his book was published in 1932, taxi dance halls were often front page stories in the local press. They were under attack. Though not defending them Cressey sought to assess both the positive and negative functions served by these organizations. He found it difficult to retain his scholarly bearing in the face of the tabloid sensationalism associated with the topic. In an interview with the Chicago *Daily Times* on May 4, 1932, he told reporters that he viewed these dance halls as serving a need for "social misfits," and that rather than abolishing them, they should be "better supervised."

Life beyond the Dance Hall

After completing his master's degree at the University of Chicago in 1929, Cressey secured a teaching post at Evansville College in Indiana. He was also employed by the Evansville Council of Social Agencies. It was at Evansville that he completed converting his thesis into the book, *The Taxi Dance Hall*. However, he appeared to be under some pressure at Evansville College to distance himself from the work, given the nature of his research. In August of 1931, he wrote to his editor at the University of Chicago Press suggesting that the term "dance hall girl" should not find a place in the book title:

> The public is all too eager to make the wrong inference, and especially for those who only hear of the book and do not read it I fear the damage will be almost irreparable. From my own interest, professionally, I fear that even at best the book will be more of a handicap than a help....
>
> During my years at Evansville College I have been under some embarrassment because of the nature of my research work at Chicago. While the president there [Evansville] has not had his faith shaken in me personally he had the feeling that, with popular prejudices as they exist, such a book published by one of his faculty would be a liability rather than a help. These conditions, no doubt more serious in some parts of the country than in others, nevertheless seem to me to be a serious consideration for one seeking to go on in educational work. However, it may be that my own impressions are based too much upon my own experiences with the more prurient among the graduate students at Chicago a few years ago [Cressey to Laing, 1931].

Like Nels Anderson, Cressey was writing in the shadow of W.I. Thomas. Both were fearful for their careers. Can they write about this subject matter without its contaminating themselves and their identities? Looking around them at a university filled with the righteous—the children and grandchildren of ministers and churchmen, this question was bound to be raised. In fact, Anderson stayed away from most of his fellow graduate students fearing that they'd disapprove of him. "There were a lot of them who wouldn't mix with me anyway because I belonged to a different social strata. They didn't know anything about my past but they knew I wasn't lily white like them" (Interview with Nels Anderson, August 24, 1981).

In 1931 Cressey joined Frederick Thrasher at New York University, where he found part-time teaching work, and served with him as associate director of the Boys' Club study until 1934. Thrasher, who had authored another Chicago monograph, *The Gang* (1927), had been a classmate and a distant friend. Cressey became responsible for helping to graft on a motion picture study to the main one. Part of this was in response to Payne Fund sponsorship of a comprehensive social science investigation of the impact of motion pictures on children's' lives in the United States.

The Payne Fund had made extensive use of Chicago school scholars to research this modern phenomenon. It was the intention of this endeavor to dissect this issue and to contract out components of the study to various social scientists (Jowett, Jarvie, Fuller, 1996, p. 10). Cressey's findings are viewed as a central piece of this work and a bridge to modern research techniques.

Between 1934 and 1937 Cressey taught at Dana College in Newark, New Jersey. He completed his dissertation on the impact of motion pictures on children in 1942, and continued working as an adjunct at New York University. After this he went from job to job, first working as a public opinion analyst with the Office of War Information for a year then teaching as an adjunct at various colleges (including Cornell), and finally returning to the field of social work. He secured a position as the executive director of the Social Welfare Council of the Oranges and Maplewood, New Jersey. Although this was not his dream job, it allowed him to continue to do adjunct teaching. He was now forty-three years of age. It appeared as though Cressey would never truly find a home in the academy.

His wife, Germaine Poreau, had a teaching position at Montclair State

Teacher's College. She was eventually made head of the languages department there. She and Paul Cressey settled into their home at 45 Fairfield Street in Upper Montclair, New Jersey, and Cressey spent the next seven years working in the social services field. They had no children.

In the summer of 1950 Paul Cressey was offered a full time faculty post at Ohio Wesleyan University in Delaware, Ohio. He was hired to teach social research and community organization courses. He would use the experience gained from social welfare administration in helping to establish community welfare services in the area surrounding the university. While not perfect, it was a long awaited realization of a full time university position. For Cressey, it finally seemed that he had surmounted the stigma of the taxi dance hall. Germaine, who had just established her own academic career, remained in New Jersey. They corresponded regularly and he commuted at long breaks.

Cressey had just settled into Ohio Wesleyan when he began having health problems. While home in the summer of 1955 he had a major heart attack and died at the Montclare Community Hospital.

Conclusion

Paul Cressey's work on the taxi dance hall established him as an outstanding scholar capable of making the transition from the university to the streets and back again. His ethnography opened doors for similar researchers and made it easier for others concerned with so-called bad subjects.

With the release of his study of the taxi dance hall he found himself defending an institution of which he had been highly critical, an institution that he feared could contaminate his own career as a respectable social scientist. The vehemence of the press and political demagogy pushed him to find some good in the taxi dance hall that was a target of attack since he began his study.

The timing of the publication of *The Taxi Dance Hall* could not have been better. It was the first comprehensive research statement on the complexities of a critical set of social issues and addressed the problems of urbanization and modernization head-on. Numbers of dance halls proliferated while he was conducting his study. But despite the book's critical appeal and its reviews in major publications across the country and abroad, in the first several months of sales only ninety-seven copies were sold to the public. This didn't appear to upset him.

His life as an esteemed scholar and academic failed to materialize. He remained a practitioner, which was the course for many of his Chicago school colleagues, including Clifford Shaw, who authored *The Jack-Roller*.

Chapter 6

Clifford Shaw and the Jack-Roller

I F THERE WAS ONE WORK of the Chicago school that comes closest to a ghetto pastoral, it was *The Jack-Roller* written by Clifford R. Shaw in 1930.

Ghetto pastorals were stories of growing up in places devastated by urban poverty and crime. They emerged from the personal and social challenges of the mean streets in the 1930s and used working class language to paint realistic portraits of the ghetto poor. Michael Denning (1996), in developing a sketch of this genre, insists that the proletarian writings of this era, including the ghetto pastorals, raised class consciousness in America and abroad. While *The Jack-Roller* was no work of fiction, it had the drama and social sensibilities that resonated with the literary elements of this genre. And it undoubtedly raised social awareness. It enabled the reader to peek into the lives of the urban underclass and the slum dwellers and to identify with them, or at least to better understand their plight.

The Jack-Roller was a rendering of the life of a Chicago boy who entered a world of crime and violence at a very young age. Written by Clifford Shaw, who was a graduate student of sociology at the University of Chicago during the early 1920s, this work is classified sociologically as a "life-story"—an autobiographical tale told in the delinquent boy's own words. At least this is how it is presented to the reader.

Clifford Shaw was born in Luray, Indiana, in August 1895. He was the fifth of ten children. Luray was a small Republican stronghold of predominantly Scotch-Irish people located thirty miles south of Muncie. His father was a struggling farmer who owned and worked an eighty-acre tract of land, ran a small general store, and did occasional work as a harness-maker. While Shaw started school at age seven, he had to drop out at fourteen to help work his father's farm. Nevertheless, he read often and had ambitions to go into the ministry.

His life was changed when he was fifteen years old. It was then that a minister from Adrian College in Michigan came to speak at the Luray church. He advised Shaw of the possibilities that awaited him in the ministry, and recruited him to study for it at the college. This was Shaw's ticket out of town. That fall he began taking classes at Adrian College; however, he soon discovered that this would not be his life's ambition.

In his junior year at Adrian, Shaw gave up the ministry as a calling and religion as the center of his life. He dropped out of college and enrolled in the U.S. Navy and joined the submarine corps. But the war ended just prior to his shipping overseas.

Shaw returned to Luray to work the farm, but in the fall of 1918 he returned to Adrian College to complete his degree. He had come to realize that his liberal sensibilities had no place in the conservative religiosity to which he had been exposed. In fact, he saw most religion as an obstacle to social progress. With this in mind he applied to the graduate program in sociology at the University of Chicago and was admitted in the fall of 1919.

In Chicago he moved into Benton House, a settlement house started by Janet Sturges (mother of Katherine Sturges Benton) in 1907. The Sturges family was renowned in Chicago as philanthropists. The facility wherein he lived and worked was originally called The House of Happiness, located at 3052 South Gratten Avenue, a part of an area that was then called Bridgeport. This was predominantly an Eastern European neighborhood. This settlement house ran several youth programs.

In 1921 Shaw secured a job as a parole officer with the Illinois State Training School for Boys in Saint Charles, Illinois, where he worked part time until 1924. By this time he had taken most of the required classes for his doctorate, but did not finish it because of his difficulty with foreign languages. However, he was hired as a probation officer with the Cook County Juvenile Court in 1924 and remained there until 1926. He taught courses in criminology and juvenile delinquency on a part-time basis at several local Chicago colleges, including the downtown campus of the University of Chicago.

At Chicago, Shaw had developed a close working relationship with Ernest Burgess. In 1925 he established a juvenile delinquency treatment center with the Lower North Community Council on the city's north side. By 1926 the Behavior Research Fund, on whose board Burgess sat, provided sponsorship for the Institute for Juvenile Research, and Shaw was appointed its first director of sociology. It was from here that Shaw launched a career that was to have a profound impact not only on public policy in the city of Chicago, but also nationally on juvenile delinquency research (Snodgrass 1972).

The Jack-Roller's Own Story

Crime confessions were a significant component of pulp fiction of the 1920s and 1930s (Stott 1973), and there can be little doubt that Shaw had been influenced by such renderings as well as the urban pastorals. Rolf Lindner (1990, p. 142) draws our attention to the mere chapter headings in the book that correspond directly to the language of popular pulp fiction magazines in the 1920s—"Starting Down Grade" and "The Lure of the Underworld," are cited as examples. But this work drew on elements of both proletarian writing and pulp fiction to provide the reader with the story of Stanley's life. The intimate first person narrative combined with the sensationalist rendering of life on the street made the work accessible not only to scholars but to the average reader.

Stanley, whose real name was Michael Majer, was selected by Shaw as his subject because he appeared intelligent and quite articulate. Shaw had already begun collecting numerous "life-stories" through interviews. His interest in this boy began after reading Dr. William Healy's report on Majer, who was examined psychologically at Chicago's Juvenile Psychopathic Institute when he was seven (Tanenhaus 2004, p. 144). Shaw first met him while working at the Benton settlement house. The boy was then twelve years of age. He interviewed him again at age sixteen upon his parole from the Illinois State Reformatory at Pontiac. Overall, Shaw and his coworkers collected nearly 400 life histories of young male delinquents (Snodgrass 1972).

Stanley was an interesting case, since he had been involved in a life of crime from a very early age. Truancy, pickpocketing, burglary, and jack-rolling were among his offenses. Jack-rollers were young boys who frequently spent the late evenings in dark alleyways targeting hobos, drunks, and homosexuals who were vulnerable and indisposed. While drunks tumbled from bars, slept in doorways or were otherwise preoccupied, a group of two or more young men would assault them and take their money or property. Often times they'd club their target, and jack-rollers had been known to kill their prey by clubbing them to death. They frequently rode the rails looking for their next victim. Most were quite vicious.

For many the Jack-Roller exemplified the moral career of a delinquent—a boy who would spend much of his life in and out of correctional facilities, often in the company of other thieves. Stanley was a boy from a reconstituted Polish family—fifteen children in all from four marriages—located in one of the worst Chicago neighborhoods, frequently referred to as "Back of the Yards."

> It is one of the grimiest and most unattractive neighborhoods in the city, being almost completely surrounded by packing plants, stockyards, railroads, factories, and waste lands. The life in the neighborhood is largely dominated by, and economically dependent upon, the larger industrial community of which it is a part. The population is comprised largely of families of unskilled laborers, most of whom depend upon the stock yards and local industries for employment. The air in the neighborhood is smoky and always filled with disagreeable odor from the stockyards [Shaw, p. 34].

While there was relatively little in the way of adult crime in that neighborhood between 1924 and 1926, 28 percent of the young men between the ages of seventeen and twenty-one were arrested and arraigned in the Boy's Court on charges of serious crime (p. 36).

The Jack-Roller's own story does not begin until Chapter IV of the book. Shaw has first armed his readers with pertinent background information on delinquency, statistics, and maps—much in the Chicago school tradition. And although readers are told what follows are the boy's own words, they sound more like the words of a sociologist or social worker. Unlike Cressey's or Anderson's interviews, the language sounds quite formal and not that of a young man of the streets from a neighborhood as rough as this one. The sense one can take away is that the language has been "cleaned up" by the transcriber or by the storyteller himself. No need for the informal but extensive glossaries that appeared in *The*

Hobo and *The Taxi Dance Hall* that translated the coded vernacular of the urban margins into mainstream English. In fact the Jack-Roller communicates clearly, even eloquently.

In reading the Jack-Roller's life confession the reader can't but be impressed with the brilliant insights he has into his own upbringing and life course. But it is his rendering of the dark side of the city and his involvement with violence and sex that draws readers into his life. "As far back as I can remember," says the Jack-Roller, "my life was filled with sorrow and misery. The cause was my stepmother, who nagged me, beat me, and drove me out of my own home" (Shaw 1966, p. 47).

Stanley has an explanation for his deviance. It is his understanding that the social world into which he was born and his unstable family situation were largely responsible for his life of crime. Given the psychological and physical abuse to which he was subjected at home, he found solace at age six in leaving home, skipping school, and spending his time on West Madison Street—sometimes roaming there late at night, begging, stealing food, and sleeping curled up under a doorstep until he was finally carted off to jail (p.55).

We learn from Stanley that his older stepbrother and his stepbrother's friend taught him how to steal. His mother often put the boys up to it. Yet she blamed him for corrupting her children. At home he was frequently tied to a chair and beaten, and often tied to his bed at night to prevent him from running away. And it can be little wonder that the city streets would become a place of refuge:

> I would romp back to our old home and neighborhood, and then down to West Madison Street and the Loop. I would gaze at the movie houses, restaurants, poolrooms, and at the human wreckage that made its uncertain and guideless way along West Madison Street. Their conversations and carefree personalities appealed to my childish imagination [p. 56].

Stanley was only eight years old when he was finally sent to the detention home. There he came into contact with boys who were much older and already seasoned in the ways of crime. "It was a novelty to learn that there were so many crimes and ways of stealing that I had never heard about" (p.58). Running away from home and taking to the streets had become habitual.

In subsequent chapters we find Stanley in and out of reform school but nearly always confined to a place where he expanded his coterie of outlaw friends. There he learned new tricks of the trade, and became well known to prison guards and inmates. By the time he was ten he had been incarcerated thirteen times at the Chicago Parental School.

Eventually Stanley was deemed incorrigible and was remanded by a judge to the Saint Charles School for Boys located in Kane County, Illinois, in the Fox River Valley, which was thirty-eight miles west of Chicago. The Saint Charles School was located on twelve hundred picturesque acres—a place nationally renowned for its beauty and its modern facilities. He entered this institution on his tenth birthday (p. 65). He spent sixteen months there and was forced to adhere to a military code of behavior—one that included regular drills, and sadistic punishments by guards and inmate "captains"—before he was paroled. Stanley observed a considerable degree of sexual abuse in the facility where "bullies would attack the younger boys in the dormitories and force them to have sexual relations" (p. 69). Many of the younger boys contracted venereal diseases. "I knew little boys who had sex relations with four or five older boys every night. It was easy in the dormitory to slip into another boy's bunk" (p. 69).

Stanley was soon released back to the streets. But fewer than twenty-four days after being granted his parole he was again arrested near West Madison as a vagrant and returned to the Saint Charles School. This time his punishments were even more brutal than before. However, he was becoming something of an underworld celebrity. "I was becoming an old timer and the young guys were beginning to look up to me and regard me as a hard-boiled gunman of wide experience" (p. 72). After serving another ten months he was again released. In total Stanley served fifty months at Saint Charles, which spanned several incarcerations there. Each release resulted in a series of new adventures.

Much of his time on the outside was spent with friends and associates he made along West Madison and South State Street:

> Men of all nationalities and races, from the four corners of the earth, were there and brushed shoulders with crooks and gunmen of the underworld. They were all attracted there, as I was, by cheap movies, flophouses, cheap hashhouses, and, most of all, by the human derelicts that make West Madison Street what it is.... All the old bums and human wrecks were my family.... The brotherhood was made up of ordinary "bos," pickpockets, panhandlers, petty thieves, "jack-rollers," and other wrecks that compose the underworld. Here was my favorite haunt, because my friends made their rendezvous there. It seemed to me that here the lights gleamed brighter, the lures were stronger, and that there were more bums to hide me from the stares of snobbish people [p. 80].

Stanley's life outside the institution was a remarkably adventurous one. He lived for a short while with a prostitute who took him in and cared for him. While he sometimes attempted to get a straight factory job, these did not last. The lure of the street and a quick dollar were irresistible. Most of his time was spent on the street hustling, sleeping in vacant houses, alleys, all night movie houses, poolrooms, missions and flophouses.

He befriended a former Saint Charles inmate on Madison Street. It was there that he began jack-rolling for the first time. His partner had considerable experience at this trade and showed him the ropes. Together they assaulted and robbed a gay man who had invited Stanley up into his room for dinner. After rendering the man unconscious they took thirteen dollars from his pocket. "Since he had tried to ensnare me," remarked Stanley, "I figured I was justified in relieving him of his thirteen bucks. Besides, was he not a low degenerate, and wouldn't he use the money only to harm himself further?" (p. 86)

Much of *The Jack-Roller* is a series of urban vignettes—Stanley's adventures in crime and violence, his experiences with foster families, his near adoptions, and his constant return to West Madison Street and to the derelicts and social outcasts there. It was there that he sold his body, rode the rails out of town, and joined with other hoodlums in targeting innocent victims too incapacitated to defend themselves. All this was carried out in his early teens. At the age of fifteen-and-a-half he was arrested and sentenced to a year at the Illinois State Reformatory at Pontiac.

The Jack-Roller brings us inside of prison and into the mind of a young delinquent who is surrounded mostly by hardened criminals. The bad food, the smells, the violence, and life in the hole are vividly described in his story. Stanley's reflections on his relationships with other inmates are presented here.

Clifford Shaw does an amazing job in getting Stanley to reveal, through his narrative, the array of psychological defenses, including elaborate rationalizations, used to protect his fragile sense of self. Throughout his story Stanley recognizes how he is deemed inferior—how he is looked down upon by others. We also see how he becomes self-destructive, constantly wrecking his chances for a good home, a decent job, and good relationships with people who care for him, and always circling back to his stepmother and lost opportunities of his youth as the causes of his predicament. For Stanley it was now useless to attempt to redeem himself. He seems rather helpless—a self-absorbed victim of circumstance, a person who cares very little for anyone else, a young man without empathy, without a plan, without a way out.

The Myth and Tragedy of Stanley

Stanley's tale is a 1930s melodrama. There is a real sense of doom here in a story that is not likely to have a happy ending. This Jack-Roller is not even a very good jack-roller—a criminal occupation considered by many to be the lowest of the low. In a sense, he is made into a celebrity by Clifford Shaw. Norman Denzin (1995) goes as far as to assert that Stanley is merely a textual construction of Shaw and Burgess—a product of social science more than one of flesh and blood. For Denzin, Stanley is an empirical subject—one appearing to sociologists in an interview or life story (p. 115). He is also a textual subject in that he later even accepts the text written by Shaw to be a portrayal of his life (p. 116). He becomes the text. This is not to say that Stanley did not exist, or that he did not tell his own story. Of course, he did! (Well, Michael Majer existed. Actually there was no one named Stanley.)

Denzin does not challenge the existence of Stanley, but rather questions the methods used in his construction. The reliance on Stanley's testimony as the primary source of his story is central to the problem of so-called "life-histories" in general. No attempt appears to have been made to substantiate Stanley's version of what happened. And although there is a strong assertion by both Shaw and Burgess that there is objective social science confirmation here because other public records (such as social service, legal, psychiatric, and correctional facility documents) confirm the course of events, Denzin denies that these materials do anything of the sort (p. 117). For him, all these records are not objective records but rather personal constructions of Stanley. Certainly, no significant interviews were conducted with the array of characters Stanley included in his story to get their understandings. Denzin takes issue with Burgess's introduction to the book in which he suggests that the definition of the situation as perceived by Stanley and his reaction to it is all that can really be known. The attempt to make this biography a piece of social science is seen by Denzin as an error. This is not to say that the study has little importance as an example of social research. On the contrary, it tells us much about the Chicago school of this era. How much it tells us about Stanley and the people he affected is another matter.

While one can raise questions as to the accuracy of the storyteller's reconstruction of events and memories, it is crucial that we be aware that the past is always presented from a condition of contemporaneousness. This is to say that such memories are embedded in the present (Prager 1998, p. 70). For instance, Laurel Duchowny (2005) suggested that the infamous Nathan Leopold of Leopold and Loeb wrote his autobiography after reading Shaw's *The Jack-Roller* in 1930 with the aim of presenting his own life to the parole board in a manner that might convince them to either pardon or parole him. According to Nathan Leopold himself, he had developed close connections with staff from Clifford Shaw's office, who visited him regularly in prison and had helped arrange interviews with some fellow inmates for recording their life histories (Leopold 1957, pp. 191–193). Ernest Burgess, Edwin Sutherland, and John Landesco met and consulted with him on the parole study they had undertaken for the state of Illinois (pp. 260–262). It is not difficult to imagine why Leopold received early parole after the publication of his book and became a professor of criminology. Interesting is the fact that although the Jack-Roller and Leopold came from very different domestic backgrounds, there was almost no discussion in their autobiographical works of their crimes.

What appears significant in Stanley's story is the lack of blood. It is as though beating people over the head with a blackjack produced no moans, no pain, no blood. These bloodless memories are quite telling. They conflict with newspaper accounts of these crimes wherein victims went into coma or even died. The victims here are mere one-dimensional subjects of Stanley's tale. Never do they have much in the way of substance. None are developed further than a caricature or stereotype—a "bo," a "queer," a drunk. Stanley is the only authentic figure, and is primarily portrayed as a misguided young man.

The story of Stanley is the story of personal tragedy; he is a child of the pathogenic social system, and a product of incarceration. This is how both Stanley the delinquent and Shaw the sociologist see it. But as far as myths go, it is a significant cautionary tale—one of drama and liberal moralisms reflecting the time in which it was told. In Stanley's story are the seeds of modern theories of criminology as well as modern crime fiction. Here everyone is a victimizer, and everyone is a victim. The classical line drawn between good and evil is blurred. The ambivalence we feel toward Stanley brings us closer to a model of 1950s amelioration and reform. It certainly supports Foucault's notion of prison as a factory for the production of delinquents.

We find out more of Stanley in the later chapters of *The Jack-Roller*, and are given a retrospective of his life in and out of crime in Jon Snodgrass's book (1982). But again, it is difficult for social science to attain any significant degree of accuracy even from Snodgrass's tale. What we do learn about Stanley is that he was indeed violent. Despite Shaw's securing legitimate jobs for him upon his release from prison, Stanley was constantly involved in physical fights at work and was not able to hold a job down due to his volatile temper (pp. 27–29). Shortly after *The Jack-Roller* was published, Stanley was involved in a foiled armed robbery and charged with an attempt to kill a store clerk. He was the gunman and had fired several shots. An attorney, secured by Shaw, had the charges reduced to a misdemeanor (pp. 37–38). Stanley was only twenty-three.

Snodgrass's follow-up study of Stanley's life reveals more violence— a charge of an attempted assault on his wife with a knife. For this he was sentenced to a psychiatric hospital for the criminally insane at Kankakee. While there he was involved in a fight with other inmates. He was eventually recruited by the prison guards there to help give shock treatments (through use of cold and hot packs) to other inmates and to restrain other violent individuals (p. 49). "After a few weeks, "noted Stanley, "I was transferred to a ward that was a dumping ground for those considered violent. Overcrowded and shabby would be paying the appearance of this ward a compliment. It was considered the Alcatraz of wards— the point of no return" (p. 49).

According to his own testimony, Stanley was eventually released from the hospital, subjected to electro shock therapy, and started to involve himself in life at the social margins—a life of gambling, drinking, visits to dance halls, prostitution, stays in cheap hotels, and infrequent taxi driving jobs. His wife, fearing his potential for violence, kept a safe distance away. The story he relates to Snodgrass is again a story of his own victimization—by his wife, his stepmother, the criminal justice system, the inequities in society. He typically winds up deserted and alone.

Snodgrass's work is quite revealing. In interviewing Stanley, age seventy in 1977, he raises a number of questions that draw out the Jack-

Roller's misogyny and viciousness. Stanley volunteers an incident, which occurred a few months prior to this interview, with a waitress at the Sunset Bar in Echo Park. He described the waitress as "very nasty" in the way she was serving him. When asked what she specifically did, he responded that he "forgot," but "she was just unreasonable":

> Finally, she said one word too much and I said, "Listen, you bitch." I says, "You say another goddamn word, I'll throw this goddamn drink right in your face and kick your cunt in on top of it ... and her boyfriend got up and comes after me see. Now he weighs about one hundred and ninety pounds, but fortunately when the sonofabitch came at me I happened to get him just right, and he kind of toppled halfway and when he did I gave another one and he went down like the Titanic.
> I weighed one hundred thirty-six pounds that day. I'll never forget. I weighed myself. I kicked his fuckin' head in. I kicked him unmercifully. He was just lucky I didn't have these shoes on, I'da killed him and I didn't give a shit. I had those light tan shoes on and I just kicked his face in and his head and I wanted to kill the sonofabitch. That's how I felt because all this is unwarranted. I didn't do anything to bring this about, see" [pp. 109–110].

Snodgrass relies chiefly on Stanley's testimony for the entirety of these reconstructions. While no court records, hospital records, or interviews with third parties were ever used here, neither were these used to confirm most of Stanley's narrative, which was accepted by Shaw at face value. It was Shaw's contention that Stanley's perceptions were key to unraveling his personality. Still, we get a very different picture from Snodgrass's presentation. The sanitized jack-roller gives way to a very volatile and brutish one.

Back in Chicago

With the publication of *The Jack-Roller*, Shaw's career was moving rapidly ahead. In the book he painted a portrait of a rehabilitated young man—one whose feet were firmly planted on the straight and narrow road. For the first few years after his release from prison Stanley was seemingly doing well. "Furthermore," says Shaw, "he has developed interests and a philosophy of life which are in keeping with the standards of conventional society" (Shaw 1966, p. 183). Snodgrass certainly sees this as an exaggeration.

Nevertheless, the national media accepted this notion as did much of academia. While many understood the testimony to be self-promotional boastings of the delinquent, the book was a fascinating read, and Shaw was credited with exceptional investigative fieldwork, plus an extraordinary ability to draw the reader into a narrative. While *The Jack-Roller* was only one of his many case studies of delinquent boys, it was the most important for a number of reasons. While the method gave it a special place in the annals of sociological discourse, the longitudinal breadth and the color of the prose made it into a popular work of literature.

The idea of *life history* was a particular type of case study that had been used successfully in social work for some time. In this way *The Jack-Roller* is a distant relative to the other Chicago works that came before it. W.I. Thomas, Nels Anderson, and Paul Cressey each used qualitative approaches and each delved into dark recesses and intimacies where sociologists were often reluctant to go. While the methods might have set their work apart from others who were doing sociology at the time, the sensationalistic subject matter was particularly intriguing. These were subjects that had already appeared in the tabloids and had become part of the popular culture. There were songs, novels, plays, movies, and short stories written about these skid row archetypes. The jack-roller was already known by reputation. Now the reader got to examine his life on a very personal level.

Like Jacob Riis who came before them, or Weegee who came after, these Chicago sociologists were like photographers unearthing the messiness of urban landscape, and frequently molding their narratives into morality tales. They were like Lewis Hine or Berenice Abbott whose images told stories of an America hidden from the middle classes—stories that made the bourgeoisie uncomfortable and that called out for reform.

Shaw and his coworker (and sometimes coauthor), Henry McKay, had a profound influence on the field of American criminology. While Shaw had transcribed literally dozens of these case histories during his career as a criminologist, only *The Jack-Roller* appeared to take on a life of its own. Criminal celebrity in the popular press had a lot to do with the success of this particular subject. Extensively reviewed, records indicate that the book was never a big seller.

Shaw and McKay moved the study of juvenile delinquency further away from the reactionary notions of innate criminal deviance. Their perspective was to look for the causes of criminal behavior in the community, particularly in the city and its marked divisions of social class. In part, they came out of the reformist school that called for more recreation and resources to be directed to community after-school programs. While *The Jack-Roller* was a psychosocial history, it was intended to support the overall Chicago school contention that the environment was key to discovering the root causes of such behavior.

In 1934, with funding from the Institute for Juvenile Research and the state, Shaw and McKay instituted the Chicago Area Project—an experimental grassroots community organization aimed at the treatment and prevention of juvenile delinquency in a limited number of low-income communities, including the Back of the Yards, the Jack-Roller's home. It was with the Chicago Area Project that Saul Alinsky cut his teeth in community organizing. While he first worked as a researcher for Shaw and collected several life histories of delinquents, with the advent of this new organization he worked as a community organizer (Bennett 1981, pp. 211–220). Alinsky, who graduated from the University of Chicago in 1930 and was a close friend of Louis Wirth, always maintained a conflict orientation toward organizing. He had worked closely with labor unions and used many of the same strategies to help organize communities. This did not sit well with Shaw, who was more conservative and, therefore, he fired Alinsky in 1940.

The Chicago Area Project occupied much of Shaw's time. He believed in the power of a community to form a child's orientation toward life and its power to turn a child away from a life of crime. He took on celebrity status in the juvenile justice circles in Chicago, acting as an advocate for the poor and underprivileged. Although he taught courses at the University of Chicago, the Central YMCA College, and George Williams College, most of his time was dedicated to his research with delinquent boys. This was the work he treasured.

Romancing the Delinquent

On the surface, Shaw appeared very much the pragmatist; however, he firmly touted the misguided notion that delinquency flowed primarily from human ecological variables such as urban decay and not principally from socioeconomic ones. His connections to the centers of political power in the city and to the conservative wing of American sociology at Chicago did not allow for a more critical view of crime at the time. Yet, he rejected most biological notions that held sway in the 1920s. This made him characteristically progressive—a modern liberal.

As a narrator of juvenile delinquency his work was comparable to other works of fiction and nonfiction of that era. He possessed a humanistic approach to the subject and a concern for the poor that was common in the American culture industry for those years.

Norman Denzin (1995) has suggested that Shaw romanticized his subject. He points to films such as the Bowery Boys melodramas of the Depression and post–Depression days. Denzin urges that we look to such films as *Dead End* (1937), *Reformatory* (1938), *Hell's Kitchen* (1939), and *They Made Me a Criminal* (1939) as reflecting a similar approach to their subject:

> These films, like *The Jack-Roller*, told their stories within a realistic melodramatic framework which, as could be expected (but not always), had a happy ending. They followed the moral careers of such individuals, taking them through the three stages of the classic morality tale ... that is, being in a state of grace, being seduced by evil, failing and finally being redeemed [p. 120].

The notion of redemption sits firmly within Shaw's narrative. While Shaw believed that he himself escaped the life of a cleric, he might not have been as successful as he originally thought. Unlike the other sociologists we have examined here, Clifford Shaw jumped into the fray in order to save children who had been abused in their early years. In this regard he was not so different from the early social reformers and missionaries that he and Robert Park held in such contempt. His work was a testament that, through such interventions, order could in some way be restored. And happiness could be regained.

But Michael Majer (the Jack-Roller) never really knew happiness. It existed only in his false memories of a once loving father and a dead mother. There was nothing to which he could return. And the damage to his life was not completely repairable. Nowhere along the way is a therapeutic intervention even contemplated by Shaw or the Jack-Roller. He is deemed "completely normal" and "average." Any psychotherapeutic intervention would have defeated Shaw's sociological experiment and put into jeopardy the theory of differential association which he helped to construct. (Good boys become bad primarily through contact with bad boys.) In many ways this theory is reflective of what Erving Goffman later classified as theories of contagion. (If you are near one, you become one.)

But the need to portray the Jack-Roller as a benign victim certainly had a progressive political agenda. It was part of an effort to raise the awareness of the general public to what was happening on the other side of the tracks and in juvenile detention facilities. While his narrative was dark, it was redemptive. Stanley would move through the darkness and into the light. This was the appeal of Shaw's book. It separated this work from other noir narratives.

In his frequent public addresses, Clifford Shaw often related stories of his own minor crimes when he was a boy growing up in Luray, Indiana. One such incident was his attempt to steal bolts from a blacksmith shop in order to repair his toy wagon. He was captured in the act by the blacksmith, who lifted him and held him upside down by his heels, shaking the bolts from his pockets. Eventually, the blacksmith forgave him and helped to repair the wagon. But this was the type of morality tale Shaw would often share with his Chicago audience (Snodgrass 1972, p. 130). There was nostalgia here, a romance with a time when life was simpler.

Shaw died in 1957, when many of the theories surrounding his work seemed to have held great currency. By the mid and late 1960s things changed. Popular events (including civil rights and ghettoization in the north) were to radicalize much American social theory, including theories of criminal behavior.

Conclusion

In October of 1995 a conference entitled "Clifford Shaw on Delinquency and Community" was held at the University of Chicago to commemorate the hundredth anniversary of Shaw's birth. While many of the scholars present spoke about the contributions Shaw made to the field of sociology, others spoke of the social changes that have taken place since the publication of The Jack-Roller in 1930. Certainly, demographic changes and the increases in violence were high on the agenda.

On one panel, Gerald Suttles, a renowned urban sociologist at the University of Chicago and author of The Social Order of the Slum (1968), spoke of Clifford Shaw's desire to change perceptions of the delinquent of that time. But then he spoke of Shaw's "rewriting" of Stanley. "Stanley couldn't have written that beautiful passage" (one that people had quoted from *The Jack-Roller* the day before). Suttles then said that he had no doubt that Shaw had rewritten many of the life histories he presented to the public. Of course, it would be in keeping with the Chicago school tradition to modify such transcriptions. He went on to ask Shaw's son, who was sitting in the room, whether or not his father had read a lot of novels (transcript of conference prepared by Sara Vlajcic, 1995).While an answer was never given, it can be assumed that Shaw was as plugged into the culture as anyone else. Working with juveniles necessitated that he be somewhat familiar with popular culture and the language of the streets.

In his work on American documentary expression, William Stott (1973) notes that true confession pulp magazines, such as *True Detective, True Romance, True Story*, provided an important venue for first-person criminal narrative confessions (pp. 40–42). During the 1920s and early 1930s these pulps used the *vicarious method* as means of expanding their sales and drawing in readers. Stott describes Robert E. Burns' groundbreaking story, *I Am a Fugitive from a Georgia Chain Gang*, which appeared in *True Detective Mysteries* from January to June 1931, as "in part authentic documentary" (p. 41). This was an autobiographical tale supposedly written by Burns but in actuality was told to a squad of writers working for the magazine. Macfadden Publications (that published this magazine and other confession pulps) was a "true story factory," and pumped out confessions on a "literary assembly line" with a bullpen of writers, each of whom specialized in ways of making the stories more enticing (p. 43). Stott sees social protest films of the 1930s as having derived from this and other similar stories (p. 42).

Shaw gave all of his royalties from the book to Michael Majer, who died in 1982. According to Snodgrass (1982, p. 173), Majer had been hospitalized with a growth near his left eye in October of 1981. The tumor was diagnosed as cancerous and surgically removed. There was great optimism that he'd make a full recovery. But the following January cancer returned, disabling him and forcing him to bed. He remained for months in excruciating pain and died on April 25 at the age of seventy-five.

Chapter 7

Conclusion

THE PREEMINENCE OF ETHNOGRAPHIC research at the University of Chicago was rather short-lived. Between 1915 and 1935 a small core of sociologists oversaw the development of nothing less than a dozen monographs that frequently made headlines and helped to enhance the reputation of the department among the general public. These works often merged with the popular culture, especially tabloid news stories. While Robert Park floated interesting study ideas among his students, Ernest Burgess was around to help guide the research. Aside from the monographs already dealt with in previous chapters there were many more: Charles S. Johnson's *The Negro in Chicago* (1922), Frederic Thrasher's *The Gang* (1928), Ruth Shonle Cavan's *Suicide* (1928), Louis Wirth's *The Ghetto* (1928), Harvey Zorbaugh's *The Gold Coast and the Slum* (1929), John Landesco's *Organized Crime in Chicago* (1929), E. Franklin Frazier's *The Negro Family in Chicago* (1931), Walter Reckless's *Vice in Chicago* (1933) and Norman Hayner's *Hotel Life* (published by the University of North Carolina Press in 1936). There were many other studies as well—some launched at the School of Philanthropy—which primarily were completed by women, but failed to get the same attention as the studies conducted by men.

The importance of most of these studies is that they explored their subjects not as distant social phenomena but as people who told stories—people who provided the reader with new insights into events taking place in the dark recesses of the city, well before the advent of television. These tales were related in words that were understandable. While many of these narratives proved entertaining, through them sociologists were discovering new ways to influence social policy, or at least bring attention to the challenges raised by these social conditions.

People who worked on these studies of marginality were neither elitist nor radicals. They eschewed elaborate theory construction and went straight into the street. These sociologists followed their subjects into bars, flophouses, and dance halls, and took notes on what they saw. They had a few drinks, danced a few dances. Generally, they were participant observers in the social margins of urban life. Their intersubjective approach added to the texture of their reporting. Subjects were not distant; they were in the same room. There was eye contact—sometimes even physical contact. In their brand of social realism the ordinary became exceptional, sometimes even heroic. Taxi dancers, prostitutes, hobos, and petty thieves became larger than life.

Young men and women at the University of Chicago were not generally from the most elite backgrounds. They frequently came to the big city from small towns and the rural areas to open themselves up to new experiences and new ideas. They often found the margins of the city to be exotic and sometimes even repulsive—very different from the staid communities from which they had come. But they were sociologists and most were intrigued by what they saw. This comes across clearly in their work.

It must be remembered that the 1920s was a period of enormous social change. This change was reflected in the literature, music, and values of the time. In the United States there was a newly found social consciousness in fiction, theater, and film. John Dos Passos, who grew up in a wealthy Chicago family and who had studied literature at Harvard and anthropology at the Sorbonne, chronicled the great economic disparities in urban America. His brand of imaginative modernism connected radical political consciousness with struggles for urban existence. There is much that is hard-boiled in The 49th Parallel (1919), or even in Manhattan Transfer (1925).

Cities had already been experiencing major waves of immigration and enormous poverty well before the Great Depression. Dos Passos captured much of this in his early writing. According to Michael Denning (1996), the emerging narratives of the 1920s reflected a new type of realism. Writers documented lives of people struggling for survival in the face of wanton greed, racism, and exploitation (pp. 230–250). It is this disillusionment with capitalism that helped infuse pessimism into hard-boiled American literature. Still, this was not a distinctly American phenomenon. Bertolt Brecht, who had a profound influence on the arts, internationally, staged *Three Penny Opera* in Weimar Berlin in 1928. In that musical he created an urban underworld that mimicked the ruthlessness of capitalism itself.

In fact, one needs to turn to Germany, and particularly Berlin, to see how this interest in the dark side of urban life affected the arts. Exploring the underbelly of the city was an attribute of twentieth century modernism; in the arts, in literature, and in sociology. Shining a flashlight into the city's darkest recesses and illuminating the ugliness of its ongoing "social decay" was an aesthetic challenge of the 1920s and 1930s. There can be little doubt that American art as well as the Chicago school monographs owed much of their early inspiration to the streets of Berlin—a place that profoundly influenced Small, Park, Thomas and other American writers, artists, and intellectuals who were often schooled there, or at least absorbed the culture of the city. In so many ways, this was the derivation of sociology noir; and it would become the source of film noir as well.

While Chicago sociology of this era was not consciously a part of an aesthetic movement, it was indeed influenced by the same forces that brought it about. Many of the professors were connected to the artistic and political circles of the city (Carey 1975, p. 181). In some ways Chicago school sociology was both literary and scientific. Unfortunately, it did not excel in either category. Compared to literature of this era, the sociological style was stiff and constrained. Few of the authors ventured deeply into the psyches of those they studied. In fact, although the Chicago school ethnographers were familiar with the work of Freud and psychoanalysis, they saw such theory as too subjective and unscientific to be very useful (Manning 2005).

Such was not the case with artists and writers of this era. In attempting to communicate objectivity, sociologists stripped their prose of feeling and politics. In changing the language of their respondents in their transcriptions, or even leaving out profanity, these sociologists could not fully purvey the attitudes of their subjects. Their transcriptions also reflected the prudishness of their own upbringing and personal values, which they brought into their studies. In an attempt to desensationalize their work, they moved it further away from the reality of the streets. In innumerable ways their work was not as effective as that of Jim Farrell, Richard Wright, or Nelson Algren at exposing the serious array of problems lurking behind ghetto walls. Nor were they as able to capture the wave of uneasiness sweeping over the American people as were Raymond Chandler, Dorothy Sayers, or Dashiell Hammett. Their writing was too ideologically centrist and liberal to have an edge. While a good bit of it picked up the color of the streets, in attempting to be sociologically scientific it was no match for the more disciplined work of other American sociologists such as Robert MacIver at Columbia or Russian émigré P.A. Sorokin at Harvard, who were much closer to building a more modern social science perspective. Nor could this work match the intellectual vigor of the Frankfurt school, which borrowed heavily from both Marx and Freud at this time.

While Chicago school sociology was progressive and liberal, it was impermeable to the absorption of Marxism and other leftist ideas. This is not to say that it shunned ideology. It was very ideological (Schwendinger and Schwendinger 1974). Its ideology, however, appeared to be kept in line through the Rockefeller funding and grants from the Social Science Research Council (Bannister 1987). Its ecological models of the city, referenced in some of these works, drew heavily on determinist biological principles. The city was a "living organism" with "natural areas." The "naturalness" of the market was assumed and there were frequent references to Adam Smith.

Theoretically, Chicago sociology was often confused. It fluctuated from an acceptance of conservative Spencerian principles to a neo-progressivism endorsing the social welfare state. Writers like Park and Wirth made some use of Dewey's pragmatism and Mead's interactionism, but this was not the case for the majority of monograph authors. While their works frequently contained perfunctory references to the ideas of W.I. Thomas, these writings were far from theoretical. Howard Becker (1999), who was both a student and an important figure in sociology at Chicago in its later development, questions the idea that these writings constituted a school at all. The work was neither unified nor coherent as a distinct body of scholarship. Nevertheless, documentary sociology was legitimized through the efforts of men like Park and Burgess. They helped to inspire succeeding generations of ethnographic researchers.

7. Conclusion

The significance of documentary sociology as a form of reportage was taken up by Rolph Lindner (1990) in his important work on the Chicago school. Lindner asserts that there were many scholars in the United States and abroad who viewed this brand of sociological research as journalism "disguised" as social science (p. 99). He even cites a paper written for German social scientists by Louis Wirth (1930) recognizing this challenge and defending the narrative approach: "There are certainly sociologists who consider this sort of work beneath their academic dignity," Wirth notes, "and reject it as a form of journalistic reporting." Wirth goes on to advance the case that this sort of research supports more scientifically rigorous study.

These monographs constituted early social documentaries of urban life. Although they directly didn't, many could have found a place on the movie screen. "Rather than concise generalizations derived from statistical analysis of official records, they sought to understand social experience through the intricacies of particular lives" (Stott 1973, p. 160). These were stories with human faces. The characters in the monographs could have walked right off the movie screen.

The city of Chicago was key in the evolution of documentary media. By the 1920s the city was representative of modern American urbanism. Not only did it promote a new kind of urban realism in its newspaper reportage but its naturalist prose writers helped also put into American consciousness images of the working poor and urban dispossessed. Cinema also reached out to working class audiences in the city, relating stories with which many could identify in the 1920s.

John Grierson, who studied sociology and philosophy at the University of Glasgow, came to the United States on a Laura Spelman Rockefeller Memorial Fund Fellowship in 1924. He had already held a graduate degree from the University of Glasgow and was teaching at the University of Durham; but he was interested in the study of newspapers and other media abroad. Chicago as a city and its tabloids as reportage were internationally renowned, so he attended the University of Chicago and worked under the supervision of Charles Merriam. Grierson was very much a radical thinker, an admirer of Trotsky, and dedicated to workers' issues. While in Chicago he became immersed in the bohemian and artistic life of the city. He worked as a researcher in the area of juvenile delinquency and spent much of his time socializing and observing life on the margins on West Madison. He emerged as a brilliant documentary filmmaker and eventually coined the term *documentary*. When he returned to Great Britain, he helped to found and lead the documentary film movement (Ellis 2000, pp. 19–22).

In Chicago, the social landscape was in disarray. Labor revolted; criminals colluded with city officials; a flood of immigrants inspired a new wave of xenophobia. There were race riots, gang wars, and skyrocketing crime rates. The conditions of city living were unhealthy if not dangerous. But everything was brimming with drama and much of this commingled with new ventures in art and music.

Film captured some of this social dissonance. Filmmakers from around the world, including American directors, embarked upon developing street narratives—stories of the urban immigrant experience as well as tales of destitution and crime. Biograph Studios hired an inexperienced D.W. Griffith, who produced a series of short narrative films that were released prior to World War I, such as *Musketeers of Pig Alley* (1912) and *Traffic in Souls* (1914) and *Intolerance* (1916), but these were followed by the release of films dealing with an even darker side of criminal behavior.

Immediately after World War I, German cinema, fired by expressionism, began to focus on the underworld. Fritz Lang's *The Testament of Dr. Mabuse* (1933) told a story of an evil genius who had the power to mesmerize people into doing his criminal bidding. The film was eventually seen as an affront to Hitler and his rise to power. But Lang would go on to make several more crime films and eventually went to Hollywood where his name became indelibly linked with film noir.

Chicago (or at least some facsimile of it) was to star in a number of early American gangster films, including Mervyn LeRoy's *Little Caesar* (1930), Rouben Mamoulian's *The City Streets* (1931), based on a short story penned by Dashiell Hammett, Howard Hawks's *Scarface* (1932), and Raoul Walsh's *The Roaring Twenties* (1939) starring James Cagney and Humphrey Bogart. There were many more either directly filmed in Chicago or utilizing Chicago as the imaginary setting.

The 1920s also ushered in the age of jazz, and Chicago was one of the best venues in the nation for this new music: smoke-filled clubs and new rhythms busied the night. Black and tan clubs, Bronzeville wherein the races mingled, taxi dance halls where lonely men danced with women for a dime, mob-owned night spots where the celebrities of the underworld gathered, and exclusive cabarets that served the well-to-do constituted an urban playground for adults. There were also roadhouses on the outskirts of town and dimly lit seedy basement establishments saturated with cigarette smoke and the smell of stale beer. Jazz filled all of these spaces and reflected the modernism of the city—its dissonance, its heterogeneity, and frequently its violence. Bix Beiderbecke, Earl Hines, and Louis Armstrong regularly played in Chicago and were long-term residents of the city (Kenney 1994).

Urban jazz, where it mingles in the shadows with the corruption of the underworld and becomes associated with it, signals the sense of noir. Jazz is perhaps contaminated by this world and is frequently linked to illicit drugs—a symbol for the marginalized performer. It is no wonder that jazz becomes vital to film noir of a later generation (Butler, 2002). While some of the Chicago school students such as Howard Becker were themselves musicians in the early 1950s and played jazz clubs around the city to help supplement their income, the sociological significance of jazz was never actually explored by Chicago school sociologists (Kornblum, 2004).

But jazz was only one in a vast array of signifiers of marginalization. Pulp fiction, radical politics, and existentialism also signified a sense of alienation. It was difficult for sociology to ignore these phenomena, but it tried. In 1937, Talcott Parsons published *The Structure of Social Action* that was to move the study of society away from the everyday lives of people and examine more abstractly the structures that conditioned and stabilized social life.

The Waning of Chicago Narratives

There is a story told by the students of Louis Wirth of his observing a candidate's defense of his doctoral dissertation in the late 1940s. As the candidate nervously proceeded to discuss his collection and analysis of research data and the implications of his findings in front of the committee, Professor Wirth looked bored and uninterested. He slumped in his chair, opened and read his mail. A silent recognition of Wirth's disrespect and annoyance permeated the audience. Upon the completion of the defense and after some pause Wirth is said to have exclaimed: "But this is sociology! Where are the *people* in your study?" (Personal interview with Dietrich Reitzes by the author, Chicago, 1981).

Sociology Noir

The abstract nature of quantitative research, as well as highly theoretical formulations, eclipsed the centrality of human beings in the next wave of sociology. This is not to say that humanistic sociology completely disappeared from the research scene. But by the late 1930s and early 1940s the great tradition of Chicago school sociology gave way to more abstruse formulations and concerns. Perhaps this is what American sociology was destined to become.

The decline of the University of Chicago as the heart of narrative sociology was related to the concomitant rise of rarified theories of social processes and a return to functionalism. But hyper-abstraction and quantitative analyses made sociology less accessible to the working classes. This wasn't what most people were reading about in the popular press, nor is it what they wanted to read. Most couldn't understand what sociologists like Talcott Parsons, Robert Merton, and Daniel Bell were talking about. (This is not even to mention the works of the European social theorists such as Mannheim, Marcuse and Adorno.) To a very large extent, American sociology was divorced from the ethos of working class of American society. Few people had any idea of what sociologists did or what they were saying.

Robert Hutchins, who became university chancellor in 1930, had an intense dislike for Chicago sociology and a disdain for its pedestrian research. He partially translated this contempt into animosity toward that department. His emphasis on producing an elite cadre of intellectuals who would take up positions of world academic leadership ran into opposition among the more progressive faculty, including Herbert Blumer (the heir to Thomas's interactionism) and Louis Wirth, who was focused on civic engagement in life outside the walls of the university. Hutchins made end runs around faculty, appointing friends and people he admired to professorships and starting his own college. In philosophy, to the dismay of George Herbert Mead and others in that department, he brought in Mortimer Adler to reorganize the discipline at Chicago. This was done without the department's approval. Many found this to be insulting and objected to Adler's appointment on the grounds of his qualifications. He held a doctorate in psychology from Columbia and no degree in philosophy. After several attempts to reconcile his differences with Hutchins, Mead resigned his professorship (Cook 1993, p. 193). Philosophy, political science, sociology, and anthropology recoiled from Hutchins' heavy-handed leadership.

7. Conclusion

The country was now in the Great Depression. Unemployment surged and incomes plummeted. Monies that had been directed to the university through the Rockefeller Memorial Fund, as well as local foundations, began to disappear. It was difficult for sociologists at Chicago to maintain their same level of scholarly productivity. More and more of the university's scarce resources were being directed into Hutchins' new experiments in undergraduate education. He was making a name for himself as an innovative academic leader and eventually became quite a national celebrity, especially for his Great Books idea that ultimately became a disaster. Hutchins abolished the traditional college of arts and sciences and in its place established new divisions, one of which was Social Sciences. To head this he appointed Ralph Tyler, an educator, to serve as dean. He hand picked Everett Hughes to chair the Sociology Department, despite the department's selection of Louis Wirth for the post (Abbott and Gaziano 1999, p. 44).

After Hutchins came on board, Robert Park began traveling, leaving Burgess to continue the tradition of social ethnography. He officially left the University of Chicago in 1932 to take a position at Fisk University to continue his lifelong interest in race studies. There was no love lost between him and Hutchins. Burgess remained on until 1951 but was in very poor health. He supervised fewer dissertations; and he could not be as involved as he was previously. Now, many more students focused on urban ecological concerns. Issues of housing, race relations, and crime topped the agenda. Most students worked with Everett Hughes, W. Lloyd Warner, Louis Wirth, and William Ogburn.

In 1949 Hutchins invited David Riesman, a young legal scholar, to join the Social Sciences division. Riesman, who was trained as a lawyer, had no doctorate but was hired by Hutchins at the rank of full professor to teach sociology. Similarly, Daniel Bell was brought in to teach undergraduates in Hutchins' college. In both instances Hutchins bypassed the formal faculty selection process. Both men had distinguished careers as teachers and scholars at Chicago. But once they had achieved national prestige they left for universities in the east—Harvard and Columbia respectively.

In 1935, the *American Sociological Review*, a new journal dedicated to more abstract research, arose to challenge Chicago's dominance. At a meeting of the *American Sociological Society* in December of that year, the association's membership voted overwhelmingly to make the journal their official outlet for scholarly publications to replace the *American Journal of Sociology* that had remained under Chicago's control (Smith 1988, p. 134).

After serving in World War II, Herbert Blumer returned to Chicago but things were not the same. He eventually left Chicago to become chair of a new sociology department at Berkeley in 1952, the same year Wirth died of a heart attack while lecturing on racism in Buffalo, New York.

Martin Bulmer's work still gives us the most comprehensive story of the rise and fall of the Chicago school of sociology. Bulmer views its decline as a combination of many elements, but most significant was the rise of new paradigms to challenge the dying hegemony (Bulmer 1984).

The Chicago School Legacy

Sociology noir reached its zenith in the 1920s and 1930s. However, ethnographic sociology did not disappear. Many would even say that the quality of the research substantially improved. But it had definitely lost something in the process, particularly its dark edginess. Perhaps this had something to do with Burgess's retreat from academic life.

William Foote Whyte was a model of the new urban ethnographer. He was a doctoral student in the Sociology Department at the University of Chicago, but prior to getting his doctorate there he had already done groundbreaking community research in Boston's North End as a Junior Fellow at Harvard, from 1936 to 1940. There he lived as a participant observer. At Chicago he studied with W. Lloyd Warner, and wrote up the material for his dissertation and which was to become *Street Corner Society* (1943). Like Warner, his interests were more in community and its social structure and composition rather than specific phenomenological elements of urban life. In some sense this was a natural division in early social ethnography. For instance, Wirth's *The Ghetto* was a study of an ethnic community and Jews living there, whereas Thrasher's *The Gang* focused on the street gangs of the various neighborhoods of Chicago. Both dealt with outsiders, however.

Community studies picked up momentum in the 1950s and 1960s. Some of this was a response to the loss of vital urban communities to rapid suburbanization and the postwar policies that promoted the process of so-called slum clearance. The new ethnographers focused their interest

7. Conclusion

on the social phenomena of community life. For the most part they were concerned with the impact of economic forces and social change on neighborhoods, religion, and families. Warner's groundbreaking study of Newburyport, Massachusetts, was a case in point. Warner, who was a graduate student in cultural anthropology at Harvard, published a series of volumes on what became *Yankee City*, beginning in the early 1940s while he was a research professor at the University of Chicago.

Despite the fact that their initial data was collected under a grant through the Federal Writers' Project in the 1930s, Horace Cayton (one of Wirth's graduate research assistants and a close friend of James Wright) and St. Clair Drake (an anthropologist who worked primarily with Warner) put together a groundbreaking study of the black population on Chicago's South Side. *Black Metropolis: A Study of Negro Life in a Northern City* (1945) influenced an entire generation of scholars (Banks 1996).

While a whole series of community studies using ethnographic techniques emerged in the late 1950s, several classic community studies were done much earlier. These included *Middletown* (1929) and *Middletown in Transition* (1937) by Robert and Helen Lynd, which looked at Muncie, Indiana, and W. Lloyd Warner's aforementioned Yankee City project, a series of five books on Newburyport, Massachusetts—the first volume of which was published as *The Social Life of a Modern Community* in 1941. But by the 1950s and into the 1960s the number of community ethnographies rose even more rapidly. Among these were *The Organization Man* (1956) by William H. Whyte, *Crestwood Heights* (1956) by John Seeley, *Small Town in Mass Society* (1958) by Arthur Vidich and Joseph Bensman, *The Eclipse of Community* (1960) by Maurice Stein, *The Urban Villagers* (1962) and *The Levittowners* (1967) by Herbert Gans, *Tally's Corner* (1967) by Elliot Liebow, and Gerald Suttles's *Social Order of the Slum* (1968). This is to cite only a small sample. While some are more small-group oriented, others focus extensively on a broader notion of community. A minority of these emerged from Chicago.

Phenomenological fieldwork by men such as Laud Humphreys (1975) provided innovative research on human sexuality. Humphreys' dissertation on casual sex between adult gay and bisexual men in public restrooms caused a furor. After charges were filed by righteously inspired academics asserting that this researcher violated privacy rights of his subjects his doctorate was rescinded and he was fired from his teaching post. The sociology department at Washington University was thrown into chaos.

Fistfights even broke out because of this incident. However, recent reassessments of his early contributions to queer studies attest to his creativity and talent as a social ethnographer (Schacht 2004).

Perhaps Philippe Bourgois' *In Search of Respect: Selling Crack in El Barrio* (1998) represents the modernization of an urban ethnographic tradition that was Chicago sociology in an earlier era. Bourgois resided for nearly five years in the high crime area of New York's East Harlem wherein he befriended and regularly interacted with drug addicts, crack dealers, and thieves. His book vividly describes the lives of these people and their neighbors who struggled to be safe from their influence. For Bourgois and other ethnographers, the traditional social survey, the objective research techniques can never produce the results they intend—they can never get at a true picture of the lives of those who are marginalized (p. 13).

Although the roots of community study run much deeper than the Chicago school sociology, the ethnographic treatment of subject matter and the quest for urban phenomenological understanding pioneered at Chicago give these monographs and works that imitated them a certain distinctiveness. This becomes especially important when we combine this finding with the influence of the interactionist perspective pioneered by Thomas and Mead. Chicago school interactionism helped shape much of modern social theory in that it promoted the importance of perception and laid groundwork for social constructionism. Erving Goffman was a product of the Chicago school and was influenced to some degree by work of Everett Hughes and Herbert Blumer. Harold Garfinkel, who had studied at Harvard with Talcott Parsons, also drew upon the interactionist perspective to build his ethnomethodology (Lynch 1998).

Today the genealogy of American narrative sociology, particularly dark narratives, can be traced back to the Chicago school and its early German influences. While not as popular as they were in the 1920s and 1930s dark narratives still abound. And while the noir style is not the same today as it was over fifty years ago (or even a hundred years ago) an interest in it still remains. In many ways these noir images recapitulate the dark anxieties many people unconsciously harbored—a sense of helplessness and alienation. While some would like to attribute this sense of insecurity to the atomic bomb or World War II, or even the trauma of 9/11, there was great personal insecurity before this, and there will be more to come. Certainly, modernity and all that it signified forced people to face an unfathomable abyss.

7. Conclusion

With the advancement of feminist, postcolonialist, and queer theory, the "quaint" marginality that gave the Chicago school its uniqueness is all but gone. What is marginal is now central. The guarded optimism and simplicity that clearly marked the work of Thomas, Park, Burgess, and to a lesser extent Wirth, has nearly vanished from the scene. It has taken a fast train out of town to Palukaville.

Sociology Noir

There is no intent here to force a correspondence between hard-boiled fiction, film noir and sociology noir. They remain distinct cultural phenomena. I have applied the term noir to represent dark narratives of urban life. Yet there are certain similarities between this sociology noir and other types of narrative. First, while sociology noir might not be cynical, pessimistic, or violent, it is characterized by the same fascination with the dark side of human nature; each genre is interested in what makes people tick. Second, all these forms of narrative are identified by themes of loneliness, marginality, alienation, deviance, and the impact of the fast-paced dynamics of modern urban living on the human psyche. Third, in these works the city becomes a surrogate for capitalism. Louis Wirth (1938) often referred to the "pecuniary nexus" of cities that animated most human interactions there. "In the noir city," notes Nicholas Christopher (1997), "the essential triangle—the building blocks beneath every foundation—is corruption, power, and politics. And at the triangle's center is always money" (p. 151). Fourth, the portrayals of crime and deviance in these works attempt to humanize these phenomena—challenging the past paradigms of more biologically deterministic criminology. Neither these sociologists, nor hard-boiled writers, nor filmmakers viewed criminals as anything other than humans responding to either desperate social situations or the complexities of their lives. No one is all good or all bad in noir. Society is often viewed as a corrupting influence. Fifth, both view women as sexually liberated and erotically powerful. Women tend not to be victims here, but can be either victims or victimizers and sometimes both. Finally, both are connected to popular culture and in tune with the popular press. They each resonate with the currents of tabloid journalism and frequently borrow from it.

There are many other important similarities. When we look at the

171

geography of sociology noir, we see that it occupies the same spaces as hard-boiled and proletarian fiction. It shares these settings with film noir. These are the dance halls, the nightclubs, the slums, tenements, the vacant park benches, and the West Madison streets or Bowerys. These are the back alleyways where people are mugged, the freight yards where one hops a train out of town. There is the near-empty bus terminal at midnight. The venues for organized crime: the strip clubs, warehouses, the speak-easies, the diners, the mean streets, occupy prominent places in the noir style. Interestingly, much of sociology noir takes place at night when the city is semi-illuminated by street lamps and blinking neon signs. Again, this is not to say that sociology noir is alone in this regard. But it belongs to other intellectual and artistic traditions that capture American culture at this juncture of its development.

The labyrinth or maze that often adds intrigue to the noir thriller is inherent in this urban sociology. It is constituted by the twisting city streets and the layers of culture and subculture that envelop the actor. It is reflected in the prism of tall commercial buildings and vacant ware-houses, neighborhoods ruled by gangs, decaying tenements, empty sub-way platforms with tracks disappearing into the darkness, and the twisting stairwells in the quarters of the new immigrant.

The Chicago school, particularly Burgess and his students, made much out of mapping the city. Diagrams of concentric circles and maps of "nat-ural areas" are scattered throughout their research papers. There was a mapping of race, ethnicity, and juvenile delinquency. Sociologists became social cartographers attempting to sketch out the social dimensions of the labyrinth—its mentally ill, its gangs, its prostitutes.

Overwhelmingly, women were blocked entry into the noir culture industry, or they were relegated to inferior positions within it. Men were viewed as justly dominating the dangerous streets and the stories related to them. At the University of Chicago, Burgess directed women away from careers in sociology (Deegan 1988, p. 2). Women were viewed as too sentimental and incapable of the intellectual vigor demanded by soci-ological study. They were *funneled* into social work where feelings were acceptable. Male discomfort with aggressive and independent women was reflected in much of the work of this era. There was quite a bit of misogyny in the pulps. As a group, women challenged male hegemony. In discussing the portrayal of women in art and literature in the first thirty years of the twentieth century, Bram Dijkstra (1996, p. 4) posited, "Under every apparently saintly skin throbbed the hungry flesh of a sinner."

Women and girls who dared venture away from the solemnity of the home to find freedom in the city were now viewed as hard-boiled manipulators or femmes fatales—often selling their bodies for favors and in many ways twisted by the distortions of the city. Sometimes they were portrayed as victims, other times as lifeless corpses. Frequently they were the objects of sadistic abuse, or they were seen as sadists themselves (Kaplan 1999). The dangerous city street flowed with the testosterone of hard-boiled writers, journalists, sociologists, filmmakers, and their primary male subjects. But they also flowed with the blood of women.

Gender, deviance, and sexuality become essential to these renderings of modern life—as does misogyny, racism, and homophobia. As the culture was transformed in the 1920s and 1930s so were the ways in which people were understood. The subject matter of writers, artists, musicians, and filmmakers was similar though not identical to that of sociologists. However, in an attempt to be objective sociologists missed an opportunity to honestly react to the phenomena they studied.

This misguided notion of neutrality underlies most uninspired social science. While one cannot deny the brilliance of the Chicago school monographs, it is difficult to see these works in any way as objective or neutral. At the same time, it was these authors' striving for such emotionless reserve (a way of separating their own lives from those whom they studied) that made their descriptions somewhat stilted compared to other, more creative narratives of the time. Further, the masculinization of the subject matter drained many of these works of their full potential. While sociology was indeed directed to the "minds of men" (educated men) it missed capturing the hearts of the people. Thus the advance of progressive public policies might be more an outcome of the works of proletarian writers of this era than attributed to the research of sociologists. One cannot help but speculate on what these monographs might look like if women had a greater influence on their production.

When James Farrell spoke at the book party for Harvey Zorbaugh's *Gold Coast and the Slum* in 1929, he attacked both the book and urban sociology for failing to adequately reflect the sentiments of the streets, for putting words into the mouths of the interviewees or editing what they had to say (Carey 1975, pp. 179–180). Farrell was trained in sociology at Chicago and knew both sociology and how to tell a story.

Sociology Noir

Ethnography has come very far since these works at Chicago. Ruth Behar (1996), a contemporary feminist ethnographer, adds a personal, more involved dimension to her own work—a vulnerability if you will— and urges other ethnographers to do the same. Her charge to ethnographers is to achieve emotional connection with people who are different (p.7). It is this eradication of the binaries, the impermeable boundary between the subject and object, between thought and feeling, that is the challenge confronting ethnography today.

The image of the dark city of the 1920s and 1930s owes much to Chicago school sociology, which resonated with hard-boiled fiction and naturalism of this era. The imagery constructed by these sociologists was powerful; and although it might have lacked the poignancy of the more imaginative renderings of the unsettling urban world, it was a significant piece of the primal noir mosaic.

Bibliography

Abbott, Andrew. 1999. "Transition and Tradition in the Second Chicago School." In *Department and Discipline, Chicago Sociology at One Hundred* by Andrew Abbott. Chicago: The University of Chicago Press.

Abbott, Megan E. 2002. *The Street Was Mine: White Masculinity in Hardboiled Fiction and Film Noir.* New York: Palgrave.

Alexander, Ruth. 1995. *The "Girl Problem": Female Delinquency in New York 1900–1930.* Ithaca, NY: Cornell University Press.

Algren, Nelson. 1965 [1935]. *Somebody in Boots.* New York: Berkeley Publishing.

Allsop, Kenneth. 1967. *Hard Travellin': The Hobo and His History.* New York: New American Library.

Anderson, Nels. 1975. *The American Hobo: An Autobiography.* Leiden, Netherlands: E. J. Brill.

_____. 1931. *The Milk and Honey Route: A Handbook for Hoboes.* New York: Vanguard.

_____. 1923. *The Hobo: Sociology of the Homeless Man.* Chicago: University of Chicago Press.

Atlas, James. 2000. *Bellow: A Biography.* New York: Random House.

Auerbach, Jonathan. 1996. *Male Call: Becoming Jack London.* Durham, NC: Duke University Press.

Baker, Paul J. 1973. The life histories of W.I. Thomas and Robert E. Park. *American Journal of Sociology* 79, no. 1: 243–260.

Balfe, Judith Huggins. 1981. W.I. Thomas and the sociology of sex differences. *The Journal of the History of Sociology* 3, no. 2: 20–42.

Banks, William. 1996. *Black Intellectuals: Race and Responsibility in American Life.* New York: W.W. Norton.

Bannister, Robert C. 1987. *Sociology and Scientism: The American Quest for Objectivity, 1880-1940.* Chapel Hill: The University of North Carolina Press.

Beck, Frank O. 2000 [1955]. *Hobohemia.* Chicago: Charles H. Kerr.

Bibliography

Becker, Howard S. 1999. The Chicago school, so-called. *Qualitative Sociology*, vol. 22: 1.

Behr, Ruth. 1996. *The Vulnerable Observer: Anthropology that Breaks Your Heart.* Boston: Beacon Press.

Bennett, James. 1981. *Oral History and Delinquency: The Rhetoric of Criminology.* Chicago: University of Chicago Press.

Biesen, Sheri Chinen. 2005. *Blackout: World War II and the Origins of Film Noir.* Baltimore: Johns Hopkins University Press.

Blee, Kathleen M.1991. *Women of the Klan: Racism and Gender in the 1920s.* Berkeley: University of California Press.

Borde, Raymond, and Etienne Chaumeton. 2002. *A Panorama of American Film Noir 1941-1953.* Trans. by Paul Hammond. San Francisco: City Light Books.

Bourdieu, Pierre. 1984. *Distinction: A Social Critique of the Judgement of Taste.* Trans. by Richard Nice. Cambridge, MA: Harvard University Press.

Bradbury, Malcolm, and James McFarlane. 1976. The name and nature of modernism. In M. Bradbury and J. McFarlane, eds., *Modernism: A Guide to European Literature 1890-1930.* New York: Penguin Books.

Brownlow, Kevin. 1990. *Behind the Mask of Innocence.* New York: Knopf.

Bulmer, Martin. 1984. *The Chicago School of Sociology.* Chicago: University of Chicago Press.

_____. 1983. Methodology of the taxi dance hall, an early account of Chicago ethnography from the 1920. *Urban Life* 12, no. 1.

Burgess, Ernest. 1955. Can potential delinquents be identified scientifically? *Twenty-fourth Annual Governor's Conference on Youth and Community Service.* Springfield, IL: Youth Commission.

Burns, Roger A. 1987. The Damndest Radical: The Life and Work of Ben Reitman, Chicago's Celebrated Social Reformer, Hobo King, and Whorehouse Physician. Urbana: University of Illinois Press.

_____. 1980. *Knights of the Road: A Hobo History.* New York: Metheun.

Bussey, Gertrude, and Margaret Tims. 1980. *Pioneers for Peace: Women's International League for Peace and Freedom, 1915-1965.* Oxford, England: Alden Press.

Butler, David. 2002. *Jazz Noir: Listening to Music from Phantom Lady to the Last Seduction.* Westport, CN: Praeger.

Cappetti, Carla. 1993. *Writing Chicago: Modernism, Ethnography and the Novel.* New York: Columbia University Press.

Carey, James. T. 1975. *Sociology and Public Affairs: The Chicago School.* Beverly Hills, CA: Sage Publications.

Chauncey, George. 1994. *Gay New York: Gender, Urban Culture, and the Making of the Gay Male World, 1890-1940.* New York: Basic Books.

Christakes, George. 1978. *Albion Small.* Boston: Twayne.

Christopher, Nicholas. 1997. *Somewhere in the Night: Film Noir and the American City.* New York: The Free Press.

Bibliography

Cook, Gary. 1993. *George Herbert Mead: The Making of a Social Pragmatist*. Urbana, IL: University of Illinois Press.

Copjec, Joan, ed. 1993. Introduction in *Shades of Noir*. New York: Verso.

Coser, Lewis. 1977. *Masters of Sociological Thought: Ideas in Historical and Social Context*, 2nd ed. New York: Harcourt, Brace, Jovanovich.

Cressey, Paul G. 1968. *The Taxi Dance Hall*. New York: Greenwood Press. [Originally published 1932, Chicago: University of Chicago Press.]

Davis, Mike. 1992. *City of Quartz*. New York: Vintage Books.

Deegan, Mary Jo. 1986. *Jane Addams and the Men of the Chicago School*. New Brunswick NJ: Transaction Books.

Denning, Michael. 1987. *Mechanic Accents: Dime Novels and Working Class Culture in America*. New York: Verso.

_____. 1996. *The Cultural Front*. New York: Verso.

Denzin, Norman K. 1995. Stanley and Clifford: undoing an interactionist text. *Current Sociology* 43, nos. 2–3.

Depastino, Todd. 2003. *Citizen Hobo: How a Century of Homelessness Shaped America*. Chicago: University of Chicago Press.

Dijstra, Bran. 1996. *Evil Sisters: The Threat of Female Sexuality and the Cult of Manhood*. New York: Knopf.

Dillon, John. 1912. *From Dance Hall to White Slavery*. Chicago: Charles C. Thompson.

Donohue, H.E.F. 1964. *Conversations with Nelson Algren*. New York: Hill and Wang.

Drew, Bettina. 1989. *Nelson Algren: A Life on the Wild Side*. New York: Putnam's.

Dubin, Steven C. 1983. The moral continuum of deviancy research Chicago sociologists and the dance hall. *Urban Life* 12, no. 1 (April).

Duchowny, Laurel. 2005. Life plus 99 years. *Journal of Contemporary Criminal Justice* 21, no. 4 (November).

Duncan, Paul. 2000. *Noir Fiction: Dark Highways*. North Pomfret, VT: Trafalgar Square Publishing.

Ellis, Jack, 2000, *John Grierson: Life, Contributions, Influence*. Carbondale, IL: Southern Illinois University Press.

Etulain, Richard W., ed. 1979. *Jack London on the Road: The Tramp Diary and Other Hobo Writings*. Logan, Utah: Utah State University Press.

Evans, Richard J. 1998. *Tales from the German Underworld*. New Haven, CN: Yale University Press.

Fabre, Michel. 1973. *The Unfinished Quest of Richard Wright*. Trans. by I. Bazum. New York: William Morris.

Faderman, Lillian. 2000. *To Believe in Women: What Lesbians Have Done for America, A History*. Boston, MA: Mariner Books.

Firestone, Harold. 1976. Victims of Change: Juvenile Delinquents in American Society. Westport, CN: Greenwood Press.

Firth, Raymond. 1957. Introduction: Malinowski as scientist and man. In *Man and Culture: An Evaluation of the Work of Bronislaw Malinowski*, ed. by Raymond Firth. London: Routledge and Kegan Paul.

Bibliography

Forter, Greg. 2000. *Murdering Masculinities: Fantasies of Gender and Violence in the American Crime Novel.* New York: New York University Press.

Foucault, Michel. 1978. *The History of Sexuality: An Introduction.* Vol. I. New York: Random House.

Fraris, Robert E.L. 1969. In memoriam: Paul F. Cressey 1899–1969. *American. Sociologist* 4.

Freeland, David. 2006. Last dance at the Orpheum. *New York Press* 18:32.

Fritzsche, Peter. 1996. *Reading Berlin 1900.* Cambridge, MA: Harvard University Press.

_____. 1994. Vagabond in the fugitive city: Hans Oswald, Imperial Berlin and the *Grosstadt-Dokumente. Journal of Contemporary History* 29: 385–402.

Galliher, John F. 1995. Chicago's two worlds of deviance research: whose side are they on? In *A Second Chicago School?* ed. by Alan Fine. Chicago: University of Chicago Press.

Goodspeed, Thomas W. 1922. *William Rainey Harper: First President of the University of Chicago.* Chicago: University of Chicago Press.

Gusfield, Joseph R. 1995. The second Chicago school? in *A Second Chicago School?* ed. by Alan Fine. Chicago: University of Chicago Press.

Hammersley, Martyn. 1989. *The Dilemma of Qualitative Method: Herbert Blumer and the Chicago Tradition.* New York: Routledge.

Heap, Chad C. 2000. Slumming, Sexuality, Race and Urban Commercial Leisure 1900–1940. Department of History. University of Chicago.

_____. 2000. *Homosexuality in the City: A Century of Research at the University of Chicago.* Chicago: University of Chicago Library.

_____. 2003. The city as a sexual laboratory: the queer heritage of the Chicago School. *Qualitative Sociology* 26, no. 4.

Hopler, Jay. 2002. Watching the detectives: reading dime novels and hard-boiled detective stories in context. *Journal of Social History* (Winter).

Horsley, Lee. 2001. *The Noir Thriller.* New York: Palgrave.

Humphreys, Laud. 1975. *Tearoom Trade: Impersonal Sex in Public Places.* New York: Aldine.

Jabzinsek, Dietmar, Bernward Joerges and Ralf Thies. 2001. *The Berlin Grosstadt-Dokumente: A Forgotten Precursor of the Chicago School of Sociology.* Wissenschaftszentrum Berlin fur Sozialforschung.

Janowitz, Morris. 1966. *W.I. Thomas on Social Organizations and Social Personality.* Chicago: University of Chicago Press.

Johnson, Curt, and R. Craig Sautter. 1994. *Wicked City Chicago: From Kenna to Kapone.* Highland Park: IL: December Press.

Jowett, Garth S., Ian Jarve, K. H. Fuller. 1996. *Children and the Movies.* New York: Cambridge University Press.

Kaberry, Phyllis. 1957. Malinowski's contribution to field-work methods and the writing of ethnography." In *Man and Culture: An Evaluation of the Work of Bronislaw Malinowski,* edited by Raymond Firth. London: Routledge and Kegan Paul.

Bibliography

Kantowicz, Edward R. 1995. Polish Chicago: survival through solidarity. In Melvin G. Holli and Peter d'A. Jones, eds., *Ethnic Chicago: A Multicultural Portrait*. Grand Rapids, MI: William B. Eerdmanis.

Kaplan, E. Ann. 1999. Introduction to new edition. In E.A. Kaplan, ed., *Women in Film Noir*. London: British Film Institute.

Karl, Barry. 1974. *Charles E. Merriam and the Study of Politics*. Chicago: University of Chicago Press.

Kenney, William Howland. 1994. *Chicago Jazz: A Cultural History 1904-1930*. New York: Oxford University Press.

Kimmel, Michael. 1996. *Manhood in America: A Cultural History*. New York: The Free Press.

Klein, Viola. 1989. *The Feminine Character: History of an Ideology*. New York: Routledge.

Kornblum, William. 2004. Discovering Ink: a mentor for an historical ethnography. *Annals of the American Academy of Political and Social Sciences* 595, no. 505.

Krutnik, Frank. 1991. In *A Lonely Street: Film Noir, Genre, Masculinity*. New York: Routledge.

Kurtz, Lester R. 1984. *Evaluating Chicago Sociology*. Chicago: University of Chicago Press.

Kusmer, Kenneth L. 2002. *Down and Out on the Road: Homelessness in American History*. New York: Oxford University Press.

Landers, Robert. 2004. *An Honest Writer: The Life and Times of James T. Farrell*. San Francisco: Encounter Books.

Langum, David J. 1994. *Crossing Over the Line: Legalizing Morality and the Mann Act*. Chicago: University of Chicago Press.

Laub, John H. 1983. *Criminology in the Making: An Oral History*. Boston: Northeastern University Press.

Legman, Gershon. 1963. [Originally published in 1949.] *Love & Death: A Study in Censorship*. New York: Hacker.

Lepenies, Wolf. 1992. *Melancholy and Society*. Trans. by Judith Shklar. Cambridge, MA: Harvard University Press.

Lindner, Rolf. 1996. *The Reportage of Urban Culture: Robert Park and the Chicago School*. Trans. by Adrian Morris. New York: Cambridge University Press.

London, Jack. 1926. What life means to me. In Leonard Abbott, ed., *London's Essays of Revolt*. New York: Vanguard Press.

_____. 1902. Rods and gunnels. *The Bookman* 15 (August).

Lunn, Eugene. 1982. *Marxism & Modernism: an Historical Study of Lukacs, Brecht, Benjamin and Adorno*. Berkeley: University of California Press.

Lynch, Michael. 1998. Toward a constructivist genealogy of social constructionism. In *The Politics of Constructionism*, ed. by I. Velody and R. Williams. London: Sage.

Maira, Sunaina. 2000. Dime a dance, dollar a day. *Ghadar* 4, no. 1 (May 1).

Manning, Phillip. 2005. *Freud & American Sociology*, Cambridge: Polity Press.

Margolin, Leslie. 1999. *Murderess!* New York: Pinnacle Books.

Bibliography

Marling, William. 1994. *The American Noir: Hammett, Cain, and Chandler*. Athens, GA: University of Georgia Press.

Martin, Randy. 1990. *Criminological Thought*. New York: Macmillan.

Matthews, Fred H. 1977. *Quest for an American Sociology: Robert E. Park and the Chicago School*. Montreal: McGill-Queens University Press.

McBee, Randy D. 2000. *Dance Hall Days Intimacy and Leisure among Working Class Immigrants in the United States*. New York: New York University Press.

McCann, Sean. 2000. *Gumshoe America: Hard-boiled Crime Fiction and the Rise and Fall of New Deal Liberalism*. Durham, NC: Duke University Press.

Meyerowitz, Joanne. 1988. *Women Adrift: Independent Wage Earners in Chicago, 1880–1930*. Chicago: The University of Chicago Press.

_____. 1993. Sexual geography and gender economy: the furnished room districts of Chicago, 1890–1930. In *Gender and American History since 1890*, ed. by Barbara Melosh. New York: Routledge.

Miller, David. L. 1973. *George Herbert Mead: Self, Language and the World*. Chicago: University of Chicago Press.

Mitzman, Arthur. 1973. *Sociology and Estrangement: Three Sociologists of Imperial Germany*. New York: Knopf.

Monkkonen, Eric H.1984. Introduction. In E. Monkkonen, ed., *Walking To Work: Tramps in America, 1790–1935*. Lincoln: University of Nebraska Press.

Naremore, James. 1998. *More than Night: Film Noir in Its Contexts*. Berkeley: University of California Press.

Nevins, Francis. 1988. *Cornell Woolrich: First You Dream, Then You Die*. New York: Mysterious Press.

Nisbet, Robert. 1976. *Sociology as an Art Form*. New York: Oxford University Press.

Nyman, Jopi. 1997. *Men Alone: Masculinity, Individualism, and Hard-Boiled Fiction*. Amsterdam: Rodopi.

Odem, Mary E. 1996. *Delinquent Daughters: Protecting and Policing Adolescent Male Sexuality in the United States, 1885–1920*. Chapel Hill: University of North Carolina Press.

Parrenas, Rachel. 1998. "White Trash" meets the "Little Brown Monkey": the taxi dance hall as a site of interracial and gender alliances between white working class women and Filipino immigrant men in the 1920s and '30s. *Amerasia Journal*, 24 No. 2.

Peiss, Kathy. 1989. Charity girls and hidden pleasures: historical notes on working class sexuality 1880–1929. In K. Peiss and C. Simmons, eds., *Passion and Power: Sexuality in History*. Philadelphia: Temple University Press.

Perry, Elizabeth I. 1985. The general motherhood of the commonwealth: dance hall reform in the progressive era. *American Quarterly* 37, no. 5 (Winter).

Phal, Lesli Ann. 1991. *Margins of Modernity: The Citizen and the Criminal in the Weimar Republic*. Ann Arbor, MI: University Microfilms International.

Pilito, Robert . 1995. *Savage Art: A Biography of Jim Thompson*. New York: Knopf.

Posadas, Barbara Roland L. 1990. Unintentional immigrants: Chicago's Filipino foreign students become settlers, 1900–1941. *Journal of American Ethnic History* 9:2 (Spring): 26–48.

Powell, Nicolas. 1972. *Fuseli: The Nightmare.* New York: Viking Press.

Prager, Jeffrey. 1998. *Presenting the Past: Psychoanalysis and the Sociology of Misremembering.* Cambridge, MA: Harvard University Press.

Praz, Mario. 1970. *The Romantic Agony.* New York: Oxford University Press.

Rabinowitz, Paula. 2002. Black & White & Noir. New York: Columbia University Press.

Raushenbush, Winifred. 1979. *Robert E. Park: Biography of a Sociologist.* Durham, NC: Duke University Press.

Reckless, Walter. 1933. *Vice in Chicago.* Chicago: University of Chicago Press.

_____. 1934. Why women become hoboes. *American Mercury* 31 (February): 175–180.

Redaktion, Hans-Michael Bock, and Claudia Lenssen. 1991. *Joe May : Regisseur und Produzent.* Munchen : Edition Text + Kritik.

Reitman, Ben. 2002 [1937]. *Sister of the Road: The Autobiography of Boxcar Bertha.* London: AK Press.

Rosemont, Franklin, ed. *From Bughouse Square to the Beat Generation.* Chicago: Charles H. Kerr.

Rosenberg, Roseland. 1983. *Separate Spheres: Intellectual Roots of Modern Feminism.* New Haven, CN: Yale University Press.

Rotella, Carlo. 1998. *October Cities: The Redevelopment of Urban Literature.* Berkeley: University of California Press.

Rowley, Hazel. 2001. *Richard Wright: The Life and Times.* New York: Henry Holt.

Schacht, Steve. 2004. Moving beyond the controversy: remembering the many contributions of Laud Humphreys to sociology and the study of sexuality. *International Journal of Sociology and Social Policy* 24, nos. 3–5.

Schwanhaeusser, Anja. 2002. *Clues' be hard boiled krimis der Chicago school of sociology.* Paper given at graduating students conference, University of Vienna, cultural studies, November.

Schwendinger, Herman, and Julia Schwendinger. 1974. *The Sociologists of the Chair.* New York: Basic Books.

Simmel, Georg. 1950 [1908]. The stranger. In Kurt Wolff, ed., *The Sociology of Georg Simmel.* New York: Free Press of Glencoe.

Simmons, Christine. 1993. Modern sexuality and the myth of Victorian repression. In *Gender and American History Since 1890,* ed. by Barbara Melosh. New York: Routledge.

Skinner, Robert. 1988. Donald Hamilton. In *The Big Book of Noir,* ed. by Ed Gorman. New York: Carol & Graf.

Smith, Dennis. 1988. *The Chicago School: A Liberal Critique of Capitalism.* New York: St. Martin's.

Snodgrass, Jon. 1972. *The American Criminological Tradition: Portraits of the Men and Ideology in a Discipline.* PhD dissertation: University of Pennsylvania.

_____. 1982. *The Jack-Roller at Seventy.* Lexington, MA: Lexington Books.

Bibliography

Starrett, Vincent. 1965. *Born in a Bookshop: Chapters from the Chicago Renascence.* Norman: University of Oklahoma Press.

Stott, William. 1973. *Documentary Expression in Thirties America.* New York: Oxford University Press.

Tanenhaus, David S. 2004. *Juvenile Justice in the Making.* New York: Oxford University Press.

Tatar, Maria. 1995. *Lustmord: Sexual Murder in Weimar Germany.* Princeton, NJ: Princeton University Press.

Thomas, W.I. 1898. The relation of sex to primitive social control. *American Journal of Sociology* 3: 754–776.

_____. 1908. Older and newer ideas of marriage. *American Magazine* 6: 548–552.

_____. 1908a. The psychology of woman's dress. *American Magazine* 67: 66–72.

_____. 1908b. The mind of woman. *American Magazine* 67: 146–152.

_____. 1909. Votes for women. *American Magazine* 68: 292–301.

_____. 1909a. Women and the occupations. *American Magazine* 68: 463–470.

_____. 1958. *The Polish Peasant in Europe and America* Vol. II. [Originally published between 1918 and 1920. New York: Dover.

_____. 1967. *The Unadjusted Girl with Cases and Standpoint for Behavior Analysis.* [Originally published in 1923]. Introduction by Michael Parenti. Evanston, IL: Harper Torchbooks.

_____. 1969. *The Unadjusted Girl with Cases and Standpoint for Behavior Analysis.* Foreword by Mrs. W.F. Drummer. Montclare, NJ: Patterson Smith and Florian Znaniecki.

_____. 1974. *Sex and Society.* [Originally published in 1907]. New York. Arno Press.

Tully, Jim. 1924. *Beggars of Life.* Garden City, NY: Garden City Publishing.

Vernet, Marc. 1993. Film noir on the edge of doom. In Joan Copjec, ed., *Shades of Noir.* New York: Verso.

Vice Commission of Chicago. 1970 [1921]. *The Social Evil of Chicago.* New York: Arno Press and The New York Times.

Weiner, Lynn. 1984. Sisters of the road, women transients and tramps. In E.H. Monkkonen, ed., *Walking to Work: Tramps in America, 1790-1935,* op. cit.

Whyte, William Foote. 1994. *Participant Observer: An Autobiography.* Ithaca, NY: ILR Press.

Widmer, Kingsley. 1968. The way out: some life-styles of the literary tough guy and the proletarian hero, in David Madden, ed., *Tough Guy Writers of the Thirties.* Carbondale, IL: Southern Illinois University Press.

Wilson, Elizabeth. 1991. *The Sphinx in the City.* Berkeley: University of California Press.

Wirth, Louis. 1930. Drei amerikanische Neuerscheinungen zur Groëßstadtsociologie. In *Kolner Vierteljahreshefte fur Soziologie* 9 (Quoted in Lindner 1990).

_____. 1938. Urbanism as a way of life. *American Journal of Sociology* 44 (July).

Znaniecki, Florian. 1948. William I. Thomas as a collaborator. *Sociology and Social Research* (March-April): 165–167.

Bibliography

Zorbaugh, Harvey W. 1929. *The Gold Coast and the Slum.* Chicago. University of
   Chicago Press.

Department of Special Collections, Regenstein Library, University of Chicago.
BUP Board of University Publications
EBPA Ernest Burgess Papers—Addenda
REPPA Robert E. Park Papers—Addenda

Newspapers

CDT Chicago Daily *Tribune*
NYT New York *Times*

Index

Index

Index

Index

Index

Parrenas, Rachel 137
Parsons, Talcott 165, 166, 170
Pateman, Barry 110
Payne Fund 140
penny press 116
Perelman, S.J. 84
perversion 16, 74, 101, 104
Phantom Lady (1944) 120
Pinkerton, Allan 18, 37, 97, 112, 129
Pinkerton Agency 112
Poe, Edgar Allan 14
Polish Peasant in Europe and the United States 33, 64–65, 66, 81
Polish peasants 63–66, 81
Popular Front 13
Poreau, Germaine 140
The Postman Always Rings Twice (1946) 8, 9, 87
Pragmatism (American) 28
Praz, Mario 13
prohibition 70
prostitution 19, 20, 36, 40, 43, 67, 74, 75, 80, 101, 102, 109, 160

race riots 44
racism 63, 135, 136, 173
Rains, Della 78
realism 14, 19, 49
Reckless, Walter 38, 43, 44, 51, 107, 108, 159
red-baiting 76
Reitman, Ben 92, 93, 109–110
Rice, Craig 2, 51
Riis, Jacob 154
The Roaring Twenties (1929) 164
Robinson, Edward G. 111
Rockefeller, John D. 29
Rockefeller Foundation 35
Rotella, Carlo 27
Ryerson, Martin 79

St. Charles School for Boys 148
Sanchez-Jankowski, Martin 27
Sandburg, Carl 20, 23, 29
Sayers, Dorothy 162
Scarface (1932) 164
Schmoller, Gustav von 30, 96
Scott, William 158
sexuality 25, 40, 41, 62, 66–68, 73–75, 81, 84, 86, 107, 124, 126

Shanghi Express (1932) 39
Shaw, Clifford 3, 22, 43, 45, 49–51, 142, 143, 149–152, 155, 157, 158
Shils, Edward 48
shop girls 21
Shute, Nevil 121
Simmel, Georg 16, 23, 32, 58, 87
Simmons, Christina 39
Sinclair, Upton 20
Siodmak, Robert 120
slumming 41, 125
Small, Albion 23, 29–32, 34, 59, 61, 64, 79, 86, 161
Smith, Arthur Lessner 129
Smith, June Edith 129
Snodgrass, Jonathan 152, 153, 158
Snyder, Albert 7
Snyder, Ruth 9–10
Social Science Research Council 85, 104, 162
Socialism 20, 109
Society for the Protection of Immigrants 66
Sombart, Werner 15
Sorkin, P.A. 162
Spencer, Herbert 59
Stanley 145–153, 157, 158; *see also* Majer, Michael
Starr, Frederick 32
Starrett, Vincent 44
Stein, Maurice 169
Steinthal, Heymann 31, 58
Sternberg, Otto von 39
story papers 16, 17
Street of Chance (1930) 120
Sturges, Janet 144
suffrage (women's) 20, 63, 70
Sutherland, Edwin 151
Suttles, Gerald 157–158, 169
Swaine, Dorothy 64, 85
Swenson, John 90
Syndicalism (American) 66

tabloid journalism 10, 22, 70
The Taxi Dancer (1927) 121
Taylor, Graham 74
tea rooms 72
They Shoot Horses, Don't They? 85
Thomas, Harriet Park 25, 62, 75–77, 79, 81
Thomas, Thaddeus 57

Index